THE NATURE OF MUSIC

HERMANN SCHERCHEN

The Nature of Music

HENRY REGNERY COMPANY

1950

Republished 1972
Scholarly Press, Inc., 22929 Industrial Drive East
St. Clair Shores, Michigan 48080

Translated from the German
VOM WESEN DER MUSIK
by WILLIAM MANN

Library of Congress Cataloging in Publication Data

Scherchen, Hermann, 1891-1966.
    The nature of music.

    Translation of Vom Wesen der Musik.
    Reprint of the 1950 ed.
    CONTENTS: The foundations of modern music (Joseph
Sauveur)--The secret of creative art (Johann Sebastian
Bach)--The imaginative portrayal of musical material
(Ludwig van Beethoven)
    1. Sauveur, Josephm 1653-1716. 2. Bach, Johann
Sebastian, 1685-1750. 3. Beethoven, Ludwig van, 1770-
1827. I. Title.
ML385.S372 1972   780'.903   76-181246
ISBN 0-403-01671-1

CONTENTS

TRANSLATOR'S NOTE

This has been a fascinating, but peculiarly difficult book to translate. The German language and ours are not further removed than our approaches to music. Musicians in both countries, and indeed all over the world, become involved when they try to describe and explain music but involved in very different ways. What was difficult here was to render the point of the author's discussion—a quintessentially German one—into terms readily perceptible to an English reader, in fact to avoid mixing concepts.

I have enjoyed the inestimable benefit of many highly experienced persons' advice in attempting this translation. For help both in spirit and letter I take this chance of thanking Mrs Jansen Scherchen, Mrs Norman Del Mar, Mr Deryck Cooke, Mr Thurston Dart and Mr James Gordon. I owe a special debt of gratitude to Professor Dent who not only wrote the preface but read the proofs with a scrupulous attention that was able to clarify seemingly obscure points in the author's uncompromising argument and set right my own misconceptions as to his intentions.

Most of all I owe to my wife a wealth of encouragement and criticism which has throughout lightened an arduous if intellectually rewarding task.

W. S. M.

PREFACE

Hermann Scherchen needs no introduction as a conductor; he has long been world-famous, notably as an interpreter of the most modern composers, and there is no conductor indeed who has deserved more gratitude of them, for none has ever succeeded, as he invariably does, in making their obscurest complexities so clear to the ordinary concert-goer. He has already revealed the secrets of his method in his *Lehrbuch des Dirigierens* (Leipzig, 1929)*; it is simply that he possesses the artistic sensibility to experience acutely and completely the emotional values of modern music and has at the same time the practical know-ledge of the instruments which enables him to explain to his orchestra the precise technical methods by which they are to be made audible. In the course of a single sentence he will include both some un-expected flash of poetic insight and a plain direction to the second trombone to take a breath before the third crotchet; he prints one bar of music, the reader takes that imaginary breath, and experiences the emotion with a new understanding of the whole passage.

In the present work he carries out the same principle, and it is the principle on which all teachers ought to proceed. At first sight the book may seem to be a capricious jumble of ecstatic raptures and dry tech-nical analyses, but a careful reading, with a note-by-note reference to the musical examples, will prove singularly illuminating. The first section deals with the purely physical basis of music and the acoustic discoveries of Joseph Sauveur early in the eighteenth century; in the second Scherchen minutely analyses one single chorale-prelude of J. S. Bach; in the third he takes us rapidly yet penetratingly through the nine symphonies of Beethoven. On almost every page he expects us to make the most astonishing mental jumps; Lully and Rameau jostle Schönberg and Stravinsky in the thick of a dissection of Bach or

* English translation by M. D. Calvocoressi.

9

Beethoven, while Mersenne and Perrault may look in at any moment with a remark about upper partials and absolute pitch.

It is perhaps bewildering, but intensely stimulating. No musician, Scherchen tells us, least of all the ultra-modern musician, can afford to be ignorant of the science of acoustics. 'The rest may listen and wonder,' as Browning said, but 'we musicians' do not really 'know'—in a scientific sense—anything like enough. We may frequently find ourselves in disagreement with Scherchen's ideas and contentions, but if we do, we must think the relevant problem out again for ourselves and perhaps come to the conclusion that he was right after all. No book is of much use unless it is provocative as well as scientific. Scherchen does not set out to tell us everything we need to know once and for all; but he indicates a method of study which we have got to pursue on our own.

The reader will be struck, I hope, by the fact that Scherchen, even in his most mystical and prophetic utterances, is never for a moment pictorial. He tries, and in doing so wrestles in agony with the German language (as indeed his translators have done, and with the English language too) to find the *mot juste* for the minutest and subtlest shades of emotional expression and interpretation, but nothing could be further from his mind than to make music 'tell a story' or evoke pictorial images. Metaphors of darkness and light, abasement and exaltation, hesitancy and resolution we must allow to be legitimate, as hardly more than extensions of the notions of tension and relaxation which are fundamental to musical psychology.

A critic remarked once that Scherchen's personality impressed itself more at a rehearsal than at a performance. I quote this as a tribute of profound respect. Scherchen is a sensitive craftsman of the highest accomplishment and a singularly inspiring teacher. Showmanship and charlatanism are simply inconceivable to him. If he can lead others to walk in his footsteps he will have done more for the whole art of music than all the galaxy of 'international celebrities.'

EDWARD J. DENT.

THE
NATURE OF
MUSIC

INTRODUCTION

I T IS UNFAIR to call the eighteenth century the century of mathematics and philosophy. Its real significance lies in the fact that then for the first time music achieved complete maturity.

Sauveur, a French physicist who was deaf and dumb from birth laid the foundations of acoustics in 1700. In 1750, J. S. Bach, then blind, dictated his finest composition; and in 1800, Beethoven, already on the way to incurable deafness, felt the inward call to transform the sounds of music into a spiritual language.

It is extraordinary that a deaf mute should have discovered the scientific basis of music, that a blind and dying man should be the first to proclaim the mysteries of its creation, while a third, also deaf, should have given it an added emotional power. These are unique examples in the history of music, an art which Europe has made peculiarly her own.

In all other artistic spheres Europe had failed to improve upon the knowledge acquired by older civilizations. In classical times men were aware of the elements of science as we know it to-day: they were the first to try out our social experiments: they forecast the bases of all our moral philosophy.

Few spheres of discovery remained open to Europe; among these, music is of supreme importance. It is music that shows the western mind at its most creative and from 1700 onwards it reflected that marked development in mankind which is revealed in the historical and spiritual uniqueness of Europe.

Polyphony and harmony were both the invention of the modern western world. They form the link between the declining Middle Ages and modern times. The turning point was reached when, at the end of the sixteenth century, a scientific renascence in Europe revealed the nature of the earth and heavens and their laws of rotation. With the aid of the telescope and microscope, science penetrated the vast world of bodies great and small. The authority of dogma was superseded by knowledge. The power of reasoning was acknowledged as man's only positive criterion.

Through music, mankind forgot the terrors of instability. While the integral and differential calculi made time intelligible, polyphonic music gradually developed into a direct representation of human emotion.

Until 1600, these emotions looked to polyphony for expression: its plastic potentialities were still bounded by melodic line and the separate voices were only integrated by the purely mechanical rules of consonance. But the arts of imitation, canon and fugue were already able to mirror man's awareness of time. In the musical shorthand of puzzle canons and of thematic augmentation and diminution, as found in settings of the Mass, the fully developed polyphonic structure is indicated by a thematic phrase from which the whole composition unfolds.

From 1600, homophony began to take precedence. The vertical aspect of polyphony, which owed its origin to the laws of consonance, was striving for an independent existence. Concord was moving towards an important interrelation of sounds and the subordination of the whole to one central note. In this way the *basso continuo* appeared and set itself up as a second attempt at a musical shorthand, signifying the constituent notes in a chord by a figured bass.

These new harmonic potentialities only needed a scientific foundation of infallible accuracy to obtain that profound effect which makes music the characteristic art of modern times. We owe this foundation to Sauveur's complete devotion to music, an art from which he was excluded all his life. He started with the idea of acoustics as a science parallel to that of optics. He finally produced the natural basis of music which had become men's universal language by the end of the eighteenth century and which is acknowledged by us today as the creative expression of the western world.

I

The Foundations of Modern Music

(Joseph Sauveur)

Music owes to Joseph Sauveur three discoveries which proved more fruitful than any previously known to acoustics. They were: the method of determining the pitch of a note by assessing the frequency of its vibrations, the investigation of the nature of musical sound, and the systematic establishment of a tempered scale. The focal points in acoustics, the science which Sauveur first formulated in imitation of Newton's study of optics, were 'to make music the object of scientific research, to ascertain the principal rules of musical composition and to penetrate the metaphysics of pleasing sensation'.

Sauveur was born deaf and dumb. He never obtained full mastery over his voice and his faulty hearing denied him enjoyment of his own acoustical observations. Although miserably endowed by nature, he resolved, on being received into the *Académie* in 1696, to devote himself exclusively to music. Perhaps Père Mersenne prompted him to do so when, in his *Harmonie Universelle* (1636–7), he said: 'Even a deaf man, if he knows the length and thickness of a string, can tune the lute, viol, spinet and all other stringed instruments and find any note on them.' But perhaps the scientific ambition of his contemporaries inspired him to make his discoveries and formulate his theories by means of observation, experiment and geometrical analysis.

Since Descartes' time analytical geometry had developed to such an extent that no natural problem seemed insoluble. This conviction was expressed very strongly indeed by Fontenelle in his preface to the

15

The Foundations of Modern Music

Histoire de l'Académie des Sciences (1699): 'A book on morals, politics, criticism or even rhetoric will one day be considered, like anything else, to be the finer for being the work of a geometrician,'

And indeed in Descartes, Mersenne, Pascal, Perrault, Rouhault, De la Hire, and Sauveur, this fact emerges again and again. Philosopher, musical theorist, Christian apologist, architect, physicist, astronomer and geometrician, each imagined himself to be especially qualified to write authoritatively on the acoustical and artistic foundations of music.

THE FORERUNNERS

René Descartes (1596—1650)

René Descartes, a young officer of twenty-three, completed his *Compendium Musicae* in 1618. Unfortunately this work, which was written for a Dutch friend, begins to lose in concentration towards its end. But some of his observations on acoustics and aesthetics are so surprisingly novel that Hugo Riemann's enthusiastic support of the work in his *Geschichte der Musiktheorie* seems almost restrained: 'It is among the ablest musical writings of its time and it is a matter for regret that this outstanding musicologist left nothing more comprehensive on the theory of music.'

Descartes, investigating the problems of overtones sixty years before Wallis's papers in *Philosophical Transactions* appeared, stressed their importance in the observation of consonance. The major third he placed after the octave and fifth in order of consonance, while he denied the concordant value of the fourth, as being a negative shadow of the fifth. Unlike Zarlino in his *Istitutioni armoniche*, Descartes stressed the dissonance-value of the syncopated suspension. From the axiom that in Art, the One includes the Many, he deduced that the ear's preference is for simple sounds even though they may be made up of a composite sound.

16

The Forerunners

Marin Mersenne (1583—1648)

Mersenne was in constant contact with artists and craftsmen, and derived much inspiration for his research from their workshops. An informal republic of European scholars grew up round him. He was in correspondence with them all and by this means any new developments which came to light were made known immediately. In 1647, while Pascal was still making the experiments on atmospheric pressure which were to be the mainstay of modern physics, they were made known throughout Europe by Mersenne. From these important scientific conferences held by Mersenne and his friends there arose the *Académie des Sciences de Paris* in 1666.

As soon as Descartes had written his *Compendium Musicae*, his old friend and school-fellow, Mersenne, obtained a copy of it. In the same year, his own investigations on the problems of music were published. (*Opera Mathematica*, vol. I.) In this the Abbé suggests that when the fundamental of a sounding string ceases, certain higher notes, the twelfth and the seventeenth, are left sounding; i.e. the notes which result from the division of the string into three and five parts respectively. In this connection Descartes correctly noted that these sympathetic notes were probably set up by divisions of the vibrating string. (*Letters*, 1629, Nos. 27 and 106.) Unfortunately he did not pursue the problem further, wrongly assuming that the partition of a string into vibrating subdivisions, and the consonance of the different kinds of vibration resulting from it, only occurred in faulty strings.

Mersenne was a developer of other people's ideas rather than an original creative thinker. None the less, ideas emerged in his work which betray an original mind ahead of its time. His musicological writings are crammed with examples from the vocal and instrumental music written at the turn of the century and inaccessible elsewhere. Among these may be mentioned a pavane for three oboes and three

B   17

bassoons. His work also includes an informative and comprehensive anthology embracing all the most important musical theoreticians from Euclid and Glarean to the treatise of Cerone (*El melopeo y maestro*, 1613).

In 1636 Mersenne in his *Harmonie universelle* published four experiments on the frequency of vibration of strings of equal dimensions. In 1638 Galilei's dialogues appeared. Both authors came independently to the following conclusions on this subject:

Length—The frequency of vibration of a stretched string varies inversely with its length.

Volume—The frequency of vibration varies inversely with the diameter of other strings of the same material. Where the material is different, the frequency varies inversely with the square root of the mass of string per unit of length.

Tension of String—The frequency of vibration is in direct proportion to the square root of the force of tension.

For the simplest vibration (the fundamental frequency) of a stretched string, the following formula is given, where F=frequency of vibration, L=length, x=tension and m=mass per cm of string.

$$F = \frac{1}{2L} \sqrt{\frac{x}{m}}$$

These discoveries only proved useful in practice a hundred years later, when Taylor's formula verified their evidence (*Phil. Trans.*, 1715). Likewise the theory that the simpler the numerical proportion of its constituent tones, the more consonant an interval will be, was first formulated by Mersenne.

Mersenne's writings were enthusiastically received and published at once, despite the enormous cost of the 1,500 pages, the many engravings, woodcuts, and musical examples which go to make up *Harmonie universelle*.

The Forerunners

The title shows how much Mersenne was still influenced by the old conception of the universe. He saw music as a central reflection of its transcendental laws, rather than as a separate phenomenon of human art. As a result of this, we find, for example, a problem precisely and sensibly discussed, but under the chapter-heading: 'Quels sont les fondements de l'astrologie judiciaire par rapport à la musique', which caused even Fétis to scratch his head in bewilderment. Again, in the *Traité de l'Harmonie universelle* of 1627, 'à savoir si le tempérament du parfait musicien doit être sanguin, phlegmatique, bilieux ou mélancholique, pour pouvoir chanter ou composer les plus beaux airs qui soient possibles'. Another heading allows the gap to grow even wider between the definitive aesthetic laws decreed by theoreticians and the unconscious artistic creations of practical musicians, a gap that had come down from the Middle Ages: 'A savoir, si la pratique de la musique est préférable à la théorie, et si l'on doit faire plus d'état de celui qui ne sait que composer ou chanter que de celui qui sait les raisons de la musique.'

Blaise Pascal (1623—1662)

Pascal's father Etienne was one of Pére Mersenne's Parisian social circle. Through the members of this informal scholars' club, which was later called the *Académie Mersenne*, the gifted boy became acquainted with the most brilliant men of the France of his day.

Among them was the mathematician Le Pailleur about whom Tallemant des Réaux wrote: 'He was skilled in music and sang, danced, and wrote comic verses. . . . He was even drawn into the select concerts of Louis XIII, along with the members of his Chamber Music group.'

This versatile soul must often have discussed musical matters with Pascal's father in the presence of Blaise.

Etienne himself was no mean musician, for in 1636 we find Mersenne dedicating to him the sixth book of his *Discussions on*

Instruments, a part of the *Harmonie universelle*, in the following words: 'I think all scholars will approve of my works being dedicated to such men as best understand their contents. I am carrying out this plan in dedicating my *Discussion of the Organ* to you.'

Blaise's powers of scientific observation were so stimulated by constant discussion that he learnt to think out all kinds of problems. That Etienne Pascal possessed a copy of the *Harmonie universelle* on its first appearance is evident from this anecdote relating to the year 1636. It occurs in the biography of Blaise Pascal by Gilberte Perrier, his sister. 'Une fois entre autres quelqu'un ayant, sans y penser, frappé à table un plat de fayence avec un couteau, Blaise prit garde que cela rendait un grand son, mais qu'aussitôt qu'on eût mis la main dessus, cela arréta. Il voulut en même temps en avoir la cause, et cette expérience le portant à en faire beaucoup d'autres sur les sons, il y remarqua tant de choses, qu'il en fit un traité à l'age de onze ans qui fut trouvé tout à fait bien raisonné.'

Claude Perrault (1614—1688)

From the beginning of the seventeenth century we notice signs of the scientific specialization to come. But first the shackles of the old scholastic philosophy had to be broken. Before natural thought could be established, superstition and conjecture had to be replaced by observation and deduction.

It was a time of discovery, and for this reason Blaise Pascal in his twelfth year was able to write down a number of surprising observations on the nature of sound, while at the age of sixty-six Perrault, architect, doctor and physiologist composed another far-reaching treatise on acoustics. Claude Perrault had been a member of the *Académie des Sciences* from its foundation. The architect who completed the anterior façade of the Louvre, he also built the *Observatoire astronomique* in Paris and the *Allée d'eau* at Versailles. Moreover,

The Forerunners

at Colbert's instigation, he translated the works of Vitruvius, published an *Histoire des animeaux* and a *Mécanique des animeaux* in the same year, while in 1680 he at last brought out his works relating to music, *Du Bruit* and *De la musique des Anciens*.

His treatise on sound (in *Oeuvres diverses de Physique et de Mécanique*) was the first work to deal exclusively with acoustics. In his later book, he treats of such subjects as sound media, sources of sound and sound receivers. The immature state of acoustical knowledge in his day is shown in his remarks on 'l'obscurité du sujet que je traite'.

He comes to the following conclusions: Sound is provoked by atmospheric stimulation which is perceptible only to the ear, but is visible in the case of vibrating strings. Vibrations of the same frequency do not affect one another, nor do they alter the volume or the direction of the sound. All sounds are reflected by neighbouring objects which combine to make up a composite sound. Vibrations do not move in definite directions but are dispersed into the atmosphere.

Perrault was responsible for a misconception, widely prevalent during the eighteenth century, that sound is provoked not by vibration of the whole string but by molecular disturbance of its component parts (De la Hire, *Mémoires de l'Académie des Sciences*, 1716). Even this error led him to the far-sighted realization of the importance of vibration on consonance and dissonance. Perrault was near to the truth when he defined the cause of overtones thus: 'Every note is composed of several consonant notes which combine to create one sound.' Much before his time he realized that: 'Even the simplest sound is really a collection of infinite partial sounds (*bruits partiaux*) which combine to make one complete sound. Nevertheless there is always one partial sound, stronger than the rest, which gives to the total its particular character.'

Perrault investigated several problems untouched by Sauveur,

21

The Foundations of Modern Music

e.g. tone-colour. He affirmed that partial tones were more easily discernible in lower than in higher registers. 'The organ stops *plein jeu*, *nazard*, and *cornet* have the same timbre in their upper registers, but their characteristics are easily noticeable in the lower part of the keyboard.' From intensive study of the different sound production of strings, wind and bells, he came to realize the importance of subsidiary noises. He stressed the difference between instruments whose tone-colour is dependent on their material and those (e.g. woodwinds) whose sound is independent of it.

Like Mersenne before him and Sauveur after him, Perrault owed his most important discoveries to his collaboration with instrument makers. In this way he learned the cause of faulty strings, and from an analysis of organ mixtures obtained a notable insight into the problem of overtones. 'When a number of consonant organ pipes are combined in unison', he states, 'the result is a single note.' He described in detail the muting of trumpets (in 1670!) and even talks of the possibility of covering gut strings with metal to strengthen their sound, a method that was only put into practice in 1900.

The real subject of Perrault's study *De la musique des Anciens* (*Oeuvres diverses de Physique et de Mécanique*) was 'the combination of different notes which go to make up harmony'. He discusses whether the Greeks recognized harmony and polyphony, and concludes that they did not.

His mistrust of all previous assumptions is shown by his assertion that 'now that the scientific basis of music has been studied, it is time that the same was done for the history of music'.

As well as being most enlightening from a practical point of view, Perrault's *Du Bruit* also contains a number of personal reflections and critical examinations of old manuscripts covering European music to the time of Lully.

Perrault's signposts include Aristoxenus, Euclid. Plutarch, Ptolemy,

The Forerunners

Psellus, Nichomachus, Alipius, Gaudentius, Bachius, Aristides, Quintilian, Cassiodorus, Martianus Capella, and Boethius. In ancient days 'music' was regarded as the art of singing and song-writing; 'harmony' then was only a melodic arrangement of consecutive notes; 'system' was the old name for an interval; while 'interval' was the step from one note to either of its direct neighbours (systems and intervals were thus not harmonic but had a purely melodic significance). Permitted consonances were the fourth, fifth, octave, twelfth and double octave. Where there was a drone, as on the four-stringed mandora, the melody was played on the highest string, while the other strings (lowest, fifth and octave) were used to indicate the beat and rhythm.

Perrault sums up his research thus: 'The music of antiquity was only the material from which ours has been made. Their melodies had not the sweetness of ours, because they did not recognize the five chromatic semitones of the fourth split up into six notes (their tetra-chord had, after all, only four strings). They preferred melodies composed of few notes.'

But the essence of his criticism is: 'Our forefathers did not know how to compose polyphony.'

In juxtaposing and so identifying 'polyphony' with 'composition' Perrault shows that for him it was the great achievement of modern music. 'It is the sequence, relation and variation of a mixture of consonance and dissonance.' He classes the thirds as the 'loveliest and most perfect' consonances but considers the fourth and the octave to be of subsidiary value. 'Only the thirds can appear more than once in succession (i.e. in parallel) because of the great variety which their dual nature of major-minor produces.'

The attitude of his time to aesthetics is well expressed in this definition of music: it 'charms the senses by the perfection of the vocal writing, moves the heart with gay and grave accents or melodies and satisfies the spirit through the artistic mingling and sequence of harmonies which provoke an admiration in which heart and senses scarcely participate.'

The second half of the seventeenth century is dominated by the musical genius of Lully. He transformed music from a court diversion to a national art. In his *Tragédie lyrique*, France seems to have surpassed Greek tragedy itself. There is no doubt that all discussion of music was strongly influenced by Lully's genius, both in the fields of acoustics and aesthetics and in the question whether the future of music lay with polyphony or harmony.

Lully's powerful personality is clearly drawn in a description by Perrault of a chamber concert composed and directed by Lully whose ensemble was as follows: three flutes (the Hotteterres and Philibert), harpsichord (Chambonnières), theorbo (Itier) and bass viol (Camus).

Shortly after this, however, the following statement is made: 'The Masters are paying tribute to a new method of composition, despite their belief that musical perfection consists in harmony for several voices. They are now writing "Airs et Motets *par récit*" i.e. with a tune over the bass. Only the tune of these compositions is printed. If a bass part is also given, then the ensemble of theorbos, harpsichords and viols is led by one whose business is to fill in the harmony.'

Perrault's unexpected outburst is enlarged in the following explanation of the change from polyphony to homophony: 'Only a handful of people possess ears sufficiently sensitive to comprehend the refinements of harmony. For the rest it is merely a kind of noise. Among a hundred people who profess a love of music, only two, at the most, really enjoy polyphonic music. Thus the orchestral accompaniment of a song must appear unbearable to most people, unless the tune is allowed to stand out more strongly than the instruments that form the accompanying ensemble.'

For Perrault, this development was a reaction. He wanted to shrug his shoulders and put this new, for him unintelligible but flourishing, modern music on the same level as the music of his forerunners. This opinion was borne out by the fact that, up to the eighteenth century, the word *accord* or consonance only meant the combination of *two* notes, and never had its present-day significance of a chord of at least three. The musicians of that time did not yet understand the peculiar structure of chords; they could not conceive the principle of piling up thirds above a fundamental note. Neither was the idea of chordal inversion fully grasped, nor the logical function of tonal harmony, then in its incipient stages.

Jacques Rouhault (1620—1675)

Sauveur, like Mersenne and Descartes, was educated at the Jesuit College of La Flèche. After his success in court circles (in 1667 Prince Eugène was a pupil of the fashionable geometrician then twenty-three years old), he came into contact with Perrault, Mariotte and the other shining lights who had gathered round Colbert. But his real master was Jacques Rouhault, the famous physicist and the first important advocate of the then new study of Natural Science.

His *Traité de Physique*, which appeared in 1671, was the standard textbook on Cartesian natural studies. The preface is still worth reading and contains an informative criticism of scholastic teaching and a penetrating sketch of the new philosophical spirit. Rouhault outshone most seventeenth century physicists by his polished style, lucid presentation of material and intellectual integrity.

The chapter entitled *Du Son* includes only one-tenth of Perrault's treatise *Du Bruit*. Rouhault deals ably with pendulum demonstrations, later to become so important. From the dispersal of sound into the atmosphere, he deduces the resultant decrease in the intensity of the sound, hints at the principle of superposition of simultaneous sounds, and allows that the resonant capacity of the ear, dependent on the brain, is the basis of musical perception.

The Foundations of Modern Music

Of all Sauveur's precursors, none is more thorough than Rouhault. Sauveur adopted his rigid methods of research, and his precision in confining himself to a few important subjects, and employed them to build a totally new science out of the fragmentary wreckage of the science his century knew.

De La Hire (1640—1718)

De La Hire joined the *Académie des Sciences* in 1678. A year before his admission, Perrault had been commissioned to make a thorough investigation into all subjects that concerned auditory perception. There followed continual discussion among the academicians the results of which were published from time to time. Soon after Perrault's treatise on sound, the anatomist Du Verney brought out his *Traité de l'organe de l'ouie* (*Mémoires de l'Académie des Sciences*, 1685). In this work, several of Perrault's theories were developed and improved. At the same time, Dodart, a botanist, published a number of studies on the physiology of sound.

In 1681 we find the first mention of Sauveur in the *Histoire de l'Académie des Sciences*: 'Mr. De La Hire donna la solution de quelques problèmes proposés par Mr. Sauveur.' This showed that he was already a member of the study circle which had turned its attention to acoustics. But all other mentions of Sauveur concern mechanical and mathematical problems (see *Histoire de l'Académie des Sciences*, 1681, 1685, 1696) until 1700 when the contents listed include acoustics for the first time as a separate science.

In 1692 (see *Mémoires de l'Académie des Sciences*) one of De La Hire's investigations appeared: 'Explication des différences des sons de la corde tendue sur la Trompette Marine.'

Only harmonics can be produced from the tromba marina. This gigantic monochord has a bridge with two feet, one of which rests on the belly, while the other touches it lightly and makes it sound at each vibration of the string. The harmonics and the buzzing noise combine to produce a trumpet-like sound, whose penetrating power caused the tromba marina to be chosen by the British Navy as a signalling instrument. One can get an idea of its scale by playing on a violin all the harmonics which can be produced by gently gliding along a string from the middle (the octave) towards the bow and the bridge.

Descartes and Perrault and, later still, Sauveur knew this instrument, and from this knowledge they naturally became acquainted with the problems of overtones. Descartes was near to the solution in 1629. But it was not until seventy years later, in 1700, that the phenomenon was comprehensively explained by Sauveur, who based on it his new theory of harmony.

It is interesting to record the conclusions drawn by De La Hire from seventeenth century scientific experiments. He was aware of the phenomenon of vibration, and of the connection between the degree of consonance and the occurrence of vibration. He knew that harmonics were an audible demonstration of overtones and that the notes of the tromba marina depended on partial vibration of a string. He realized that the longer the vibrating part of a string, the louder would be the sound of the harmonics. He was aware of the cause of the frequent occurrence of redundant notes, through over-blowing in wind instruments and unintentional harmonics in stringed instruments; of the natural scale in wind instruments; of the dynamic effect produced by the bow on a string instrument; also, that resonance emanated from the bridge and that various combinations of sounds produced various qualities of tone colour.

The history of the science of sound in the seventeenth century abounded in clever observation and experiment, but the scientists lacked the imaginative force to see their artistic value. Vague hypotheses continued to obscure what practical experience was on the point of clarifying.

Although the facts that lay at the base of his problems were known to De La Hire, he never probed them to the bottom.

The Foundations of Modern Music

The knowledge of acoustics before Sauveur's time remained in the same state as the music. The eighteenth century liberated them both, but the most important questions to be answered were:

1. How to determine the absolute pitch of a note (instead of the endless proportional estimations of intervals that had up to then survived).
2. The solution of the problems of combined notes (instead of the meaningless system of overtones, as in the tromba marina).
3. The foundation and elaboration of the conception of Harmony (in place of the innumerable old lists of consonances that were still prevalent).

JOSEPH SAUVEUR

(1653—1716)

"The task of science is to obtain the maximum of eternal truth in the shortest possible time with a minimum of labour and thought."

(*Ernst Mach.*)

Sauveur laid the foundations of acoustics through his method of determining the pitch of a note by indirect means. This was an epoch-making achievement. At last a scientific approach provided music with a firm basis. Music could now blossom into an art with a definite background, freed from that long bondage of acoustic vagueness. Tonality, whose appreciation by musicians had considerably improved, now achieved a firm foundation. The construction of instruments, the sound capacity of rooms, and in fact the entire mechanical aspect of acoustics now achieved basic principles calculable by algebraical formulae.

Joseph Sauveur

1

Sur la détermination d'un son fixe.
(Fontenelle's report in the *Histoire de l'Académie des Sciences*, 1700)

The treatise notably shows the necessity for an indirect solution of its problem. The frequency of vibration of a given note had not hitherto been calculable, because no accurate instruments were in existence for measuring it. So from earliest times, the proportions of the vibrating strings, or columns of air, had to be measured instead of calculating the vibrations. Sauveur took two organ pipes (G♭ and G) which, with another lower pipe sounding E♭, formed minor and major thirds respectively. G♭ was in proportion to G as 24:25. Every 24th vibration of the G♭ pipe occurred simultaneously with every 25th of the G and the coincidence was audible as an increase in volume. Four such beats per second showed that the higher of the two pipes produced one note for every 100 vibrations, and the lower, one for every 96 per second.

Sauveur's ingenious discovery was the first of its kind. Its fundamental principle is as simple to-day as it was then, and for long was recognized as the surest method of assessing vibratory frequencies.

Sauveur's simplification of acoustical nomenclature shows how great a debt the science of sound owes to him. Instead of the tortuous differentiation between 'vibrations', 'ébranlements' and 'ondulations' in resonant bodies, he only used 'vibrations'. Sound he conceived as a process of recurrent vibrations. He realized the correlation between pitch and rate of vibration, and also that of intensity of sound and amplitude of vibration.

He contributed the following results: the limitation of pitch perception in high and low registers alike is due to the weakness of human auditory sense. Our ears are not sensitive enough to apprehend

29

the very smallest intervals. The octave can be divided into 43 sections, of which each can be subdivided into 7 further sub-sections, giving a total division into 301 sub-sections. The coincidence of vibrations when two notes are heard together accentuates the sound and these fluctuations of intensity, known as beats, are unpleasantly perceptible to the ear. The degree of consonance in an interval is closely dependent on the beats.

2

Système Général des Intervalles des Sons, et son application à tous les Systèmes et à tous les Instruments de Musique. (1701, *Mémoires.*)

A science must have a basis that will support all its problems, a principle that will cover its development, and a measuring system that will classify all the phenomena thus observed.

Sauveur occupied himself with these considerations from the time when he decided to develop acoustics as a new science of hearing. In 1697 his task was almost achieved, and as Professor at the Collège Royal he ventured to dictate a treatise on *La Musique Spéculative.* But he did not publish the work because of the opposition from musicians against his new system of names and symbols. He then realized that he could make no further investigations in the field of acoustics until he had fixed one musical note as a starting point.

While the science of optics has little or no connection with the art of painting, acoustical problems are almost entirely dependent on music. The reason for this difference would seem to be that optical instruments such as the telescope and microscope, in making the extremely distant and the imperceptibly small available to man, are bringing a greater part of the objective world within his range. Acoustical experiments, however, bearing particularly on music as they do, open up a wider region of the human world.

The audible and visible worlds can hardly be compared. We cannot appreciate the number of phenomena that constantly attract the eye.

Joseph Sauveur

On the other hand our ears, however alert, may hardly hear a sound throughout the day. If we close our eyes, sensations of light will only be induced by pressure on the optic nerve. Should the ear be similarly handicapped, we can still talk, whistle and sing to ourselves.

Thus the basis and material of painting, line, colour, shadow, objects, all reach us from outside. In music, however, the basis and material, melody, harmony, form and timbre, come from man's inward creative faculty.

Thus aesthetic problems of music become scientific questions of acoustics. And from this point Sauveur, Euler and later, to some extent, Helmholtz, made their attempts to develop a system of musical theory from their observations in acoustics.

'A comprehensive system of intervals and its bearing on all systems of music and musical instruments'—this, no less, was the subject of Sauveur's *Mémoire* of 1701. Several treatises had to be combined in this *Mémoire*.

In the introduction, Sauveur points out that all musical theory adapts itself to the changes of contemporary taste. He asks for a comprehensive science of sound in which music is only an isolated case of acoustic phenomena.

But he also succumbs to the old tendency to include musical aesthetics in a mathematical system of acoustics. Thus he forecasts chromatic twelve-note and quarter-tone music as possible future refinements in musical composition, thereby showing an impartiality as notable as prophetic.

The first four chapters underline the importance in music-making of setting a standard pitch. At the beginning of the seventeenth century, Praetorius could give no more precise instruction for the tuning of a string than that it should be 'stretched to just below breaking point'. We now know that this clumsy and primitive device

31

has its equivalent in the maxim of modern string manufacture that 'the nearer to breaking point the string be stretched, the more satisfactory will be the sound'.

Sauveur's note of fixed pitch thus put the whole industry of instrument manufacture on a new basis.

A fixed pitch being 'independent of time and space', we need also a scale of measurement for sound, precise enough to hold good for conceivable systems of music as well as those already known to us.

Every composition could now be played anywhere at exactly the same pitch.

Key-consciousness had already become so general that in the second half of the nineteenth century (after the standard A had been fixed at 435 cycles per second) each key had its particular tonal character. Nor could any composer escape the importance of this key quality. In fact the neoclassic, late romantic and impressionist works composed from 1850–1900 sound wrong to-day because they are performed by orchestras tuned too sharp; for instance, if a work was written in F major-D minor, it would sound to modern ears as though it was in G♭ major-E♭ minor.

The Echometer was used to determine the duration of single notes and of different degrees of tempo. It consisted of a metronome, correct to one-twelfth of a second, and an octave-span with 43 divisions, 301 sub-divisions and 3,010 further sub-divisions.

That Sauveur was correct in his attempt to create a means of measuring music and acoustics as precisely as possible, is proved by modern practice. Contemporary musicians, such as Hába and his followers, could have used this system of sub-dividing the octave for the correct intonation of third, quarter and sixth tones, while his metronome might have served Bartók, Stravinsky and others for a minutely precise indication of tempi and duration of movements, had it only been currently available.

Joseph Sauveur

At about this time there was much discussion about the indication of correct tempi, or rather of the tempo desired by the composer. Lully's works were considered boring by those who did not understand the reason for their dullness in performance. Musicians who had played under Lully explained that this was due to the slowing down of tempi, for under him the performances of his operas lasted only half as long as those given twenty years after his death. So Loulié's chronometer of 1698 and Sauveur's more precise echometer of 1701 were greeted with equal enthusiasm, just as a hundred years later Mälzel's metronome was applauded by Beethoven and his contemporaries.

The importance of Loulié's chronometer to us will be seen in the following table, the metronome markings for which have been derived from his own:

	Work	Time		Metronome marking (Mälzel)
Lully	Fête de Bacchus	Chaconne	3	52=Whole bar
Destouches	Marthésie	Menuet	3	70=Whole bar
Campra	L'Europe	Menuet	3	70=Whole bar
Campra	L'Europe	Passepied	3/8	100=Whole bar
Destouches	Issé	Sarabande	3/2	72
Colasse	Mathot	Courante	3	81
Lully	Persée	Passacaglia	3	96
Colasse	Amadis	Gigue	6/4	112
Colasse	Thétis et Pépée	Loure	6/4	112
Lully	Roland	Gavotte	2	97
Lully	Phaeton	Bourrée	2	112
Campra	L'Europe	Rigaudon	2	116
Destouches	Omphale	Bourrée	2	120

(E. Borrel: *L'Interprétation de la Musique française.*)

The Foundations of Modern Music

In chapters 5 to 8 Sauveur examines the bearing on music of his 'Système général'. In this connection, he cites a number of important dates in musical history.

First we encounter the three most usual musical systems:

1. that of the tempered octave divided into 55 commas
2. the octave of 31 degrees
3. that of the equal-tempered octave divided into 12 equal commas.

We also learn that in 1700 the compass of musical instruments stretched from A, lowest note of the bass viol, to e'', highest note of the flute, and in the voice from E to b'' and in exceptional cases from C to c'''. In spite of the introduction of H* (si) about 1670, musicians and instrument makers in 1700 were still using the alphabetical naming C D E F G A B (!) C. The confusion ensuing from the use of the old accidental names Ut♯ Re♭ Mi Fa♯ Sol♯ La♭ Si haunted music in Mattheson's and Mitzler's time and indeed until 1750. All stringed instruments except the violin had frets on the fingerboard in 1700, and their tuning was continually changed either according to individual whim or because it was the 'fashion abroad'. The vocal compass was divided into six categories: *Haut-Dessus, Bas-Dessus, Haut-Contre, Taille, Basse-Taille (Concordant), Basse (contre)* and instrumental parts were likewise of five kinds: *Dessus, Haute-Contre, Taille, Quinte, Basse.*

Sauveur twice mentions Mersenne (Livre III 'Des genres de la Musique' and 'Du Son et des mouvements des cordes'). He refers to Mersenne's account of Greek musical systems, and names him as the first to have reached a standard pitch although his system was not then practicable. Sauveur recalls his own valuable collaboration with technicians and instrument makers especially referring to 'Sieur Chapotot, un des plus habiles ingénieurs pour les Instruments de mathématiques à Paris' as the maker of the Echometer. Rippert and

* Translator's note: H is the German name for B♮.

Joseph Sauveur

Jean Hotteterre the Younger he names as specialists in wind instruments and Hurel as the finest maker of stringed instruments.

Sauveur was also successful in enlisting the aid of the academicians. The demonstration of partial vibration by means of white and coloured bits of paper astride the string was their idea. This method is still in use. Later by good fortune Sauveur found in Fontenelle a champion of his ideas, and the latter knew better than anyone else how to interest the general public in this difficult subject.

In the eighth chapter the new philosophy of musical thought is mentioned. Under Rameau's guidance this led to a realization of the possibilities of modulation (major and minor keys) and synchronization using different common chords.

Sauveur sensed that the ear could appreciate the intellectual coherence of a composition in spite of acoustical difficulties. For instance the logical sequence of ideas in a Beethoven sonata can be understood without difficulty, even when the piano is out of tune and the acoustical inaccuracy is unpleasant to the ear. Sauveur was the first to point out this power of the ear to correct sounds, when he said that the ear required certain chords which are 'the pillars of musical perception'.

Descartes had already foreshadowed this. In 1618 he asserted that the lower, and more important note in an octave consonance includes also the higher, and that the ear also perceives rhythm.

Finally Sauveur suggests that a piece of music should set down at the beginning

(a) the standard A and its relationship to the desired tonality;

(b) the compass of the composition;

(c) the tempi of the movements, clearly marked according to the echometer.

He concludes: 'Our new notation directly indicates the name and sound of a note'; 'the notes are clearly recognizable so that practical complications of clef and transpositions are of no account.' He justifies his introduction of metronomic marking (as Beethoven did later on) in these words: 'for the perfect rendering of music, the tempo desired by the composer should be precisely stated. This method of indicating the tempo is more accurate than any of the ambiguous signs in use to-day, such as quick [allegro] or slow [adagio].

Sauveur was aware that the principle of overtones was of central importance in acoustics and music alike. In his chapter 'Des sons harmoniques', he reaches a basic principle of harmony, in defining the system of chords as follows: 'I use the term *harmonic* for the sound which completes several vibrations while the *fundamental* completes one.'

Definitions are not merely indications of meaning. They can build up new meanings, i.e. they can be of value, apart from the analysis of an idea, by pointing out profounder significances and hidden channels of thought. A definition fulfils its intent completely when the simple explanation leads to a new outlook and the simple representation of a fact yields a new insight into the subject. To Sauveur's definition we owe the basis of modern music. Perrault's presentation of facts does not particularize, but its implications stretch far into the future, disclosing possibilities not yet realized.

Sauveur desired to demonstrate the principle of overtones visibly as well as audibly.

To do this he had once more to have a fixed point of reference independent of place and time. This was found in the fundamental.

The significance of this idea cannot be too strongly affirmed, for Sauveur's predecessors could only view concord mathematically, as a series of progressions:

1:2 (octave) 2:3 (fifth) 3:4 (fourth) 4:5 (major third) 5:6 (minor third) 3:5 (major sixth) 5:8 (minor sixth), etc.

Sauveur replaced this with another series, where the sequence of intervals was represented proportionally, in relation to a basic unity:

Joseph Sauveur

1:2 (octave) 1:3 (twelfth, or fifth) 1:4 (fifteenth) 1:5 (seventeenth or third).

At the same time he showed the principle of harmonic notes, in the light of Fontenelle's plan for a future scientific unity. From Fontenelle's enthusiastic dictum we can still to-day conceive how great an impression Sauveur's work must have made on the scholars of his day: 'What philosopher would ever have believed that a body set in motion, all of whose constituent particles participate, nevertheless remains unmoved at certain points, or better still, that as a result of the partition of its movement into subsections, a part remains completely at rest?'

Reference to one of Sauveur's tables will show its influence on the theory of overtones. From it he draws several important conclusions:

1. Overtones are directly caused by the partial vibration of a string and they also occur through partial vibration of the same part that is producing the primary overtones.
2. Overtones can occur indirectly, as a result of resonance, when one vibrating string sounds in unison with a harmonic of another, or when, even if such unison is lacking, the same overtone is vibrating on both strings (e.g. when a c string is divided in four parts and an f string in three, both strings give out the overtone c'').
3. Overtones are perceptible up to the 128th harmonic (i.e. the seventh octave).
4. The lowest odd overtones are the most audible.
5. If the fingers are made to glide lightly over the string, a brilliant glissando of harmonics results, (used 200 years later by Igor Stravinsky in 'Oiseau de feu' (Firebird) and by Maurice Ravel in 'Trois poèmes de Mallarmé').

Chapters ten and eleven scarcely concern us. They describe the uncertainty of mathematicians and acousticians in their approach to creative work. Their questions betray a bewildered state of mind. They were anxious to know whether musical composition was governed by the rules of euphony and acoustics or by purely spontaneous inspiration.

In the twelfth and last chapter 'On the method of finding a fixed note', Sauveur touches on the problem in acoustical research which has always been an obstacle to scientists: the question of how great a part the personal view of the experimenter plays in the work. We are reminded of Daniel Bernouilli reproaching his friend Leonhard Euler for attaching more importance to geometrical analysis than to isolated actual events. And Schäfer, the chief engineer of the Berlin Broadcasting Corporation who committed suicide in 1933, said he was glad that his complete unmusicality prevented him from ever being tempted to make acoustic judgments with an imperfect ear.

Sauveur's defective hearing put him in a similar position to Schäfer; at the same time he had to face the same difficulties as Euler. He overcame his auditory defect by working with the best technicians of his day and avoided his subjection to mathematical dogma, by reasoning that the phenomenon of beats was nature's own apparatus for measuring vibrations that could not be counted.

Sauveur realized his limitations in auditory perception. Nevertheless he assumed an exact ear as the premise for the application of his method and noted down all the faults that were bound to be present in the instruments in use.

At the end of this *Mémoire* Sauveur draws certain conclusions which well display the quality of his scientific reasoning.

He states that:

In Music—the natural frequency of all sounding bodies may be readily reckoned.

In Physiology—the perceptory limits of the human ear may be exactly determined for high as well as low notes.

Joseph Sauveur

In the Mathematics of Acoustics—the air displaced by a vibrating
 string can also be determined.

In Physics—changes of natural frequency in a sounding body give
 some indication of the condition of its substance.

Sauveur's scientific far-sightedness is well-shown here. Two hundred years later acoustical machinery was set up in a turbine factory
to assess faults by registering the changes in a dynamo's pitch.
Sauveur also had the idea of examining material with super-sonic
waves in order to ascertain the condition of its substance.

Increase in the pressure on a compressed body raises its pitch when
struck. The realization of this fact has saved human life. Miners and
sappers knock on the wooden part of the roof when they enter a
tunnel and estimate the pressure of the mountain above. If the pitch
is found to rise quickly, the roof has to be strengthened.

3.

Overtones and the construction of organ stops (1702)

Sauveur here proves that the principle of overtones had already
been applied unwittingly to organ stops and mixtures. Long before
scientific thought was brought to bear on the subject, this principle
was in practical use. The natural application of Sauveur's theoretical
discovery to the century-old craft of organ building led Fontenelle to
exclaim: 'This concept of the numerical proportions of notes is the
representative expression of all the music which nature has given
us.' Rameau was also influenced by this train of thought.

Sauveur's valuable book deals with the construction of the organ,
the various pipe-materials, the differences of sound due to diameter,
density of material, shape of the pipe and wind pressure, the characteristics of various stops, and dimensions of the longest and shortest
organ pipes.

The Foundations of Modern Music

He then gives interesting directions for tuning the organ and here again overtones play an important part.

All these instructions show the state of organ building and the design of organs in 1700 as well as their practical and acoustical potentialities. They are followed by accounts of organ registration in 1636 and of the problems of organ playing in 1665. Sauveur's *Mémoire* is thus a very valuable record of the art of the French organ builder in the seventeenth century.

Sauveur further writes that the harpsichords and spinets of 1700 were fitted with black keys for the seven diatonic notes and white keys for the five chromatic notes, while the organ followed the reversed practice now normal. It is said that this was done because the black diatonic keys showed a lady's white hands to greater advantage. The following quotation once again demonstrates Sauveur's unbiased approach to everything connected with his experiments: 'Although the blending of organ stops of the same kind will have almost the same results, there are in fact differences which force the organist to vary his registration slightly just as painters are the slaves of their own taste when preparing colours.

There are general rules for the use of mixtures. The first is that all notes produced by the same key must be identical in pitch; any deviation would result in dissonance. The second states that the registration must be appropriate to the character of the piece (e.g., prelude, fugue, duo, trio, etc.). In this, individual taste and inclination play the same part as seasoning in good cooking.'

4.

Méthode générale pour former des systèmes tempérés de Musique, et de celui qu'on doit suivre.

All Sauveur's experiments were ultimately concerned with music. The phenomenon of sound as such scarcely concerned him. He

Joseph Sauveur

abandoned his original intention, to establish a general system of sound in which music was only a particular case. His investigations were eventually directed towards a musical system in which acoustics served as a scientific basis.

The law of the inversion of intervals could now be formulated with scientific accuracy. Once the smaller intervals (from unison to fourth) were fixed, he could deduce the correspondingly larger ones (fifth to octave).

This knowledge, with the previously formed concept of tonality, provided the essential hypothesis for Rameau's law of chordal inversion. Modern musical theory begins with this limitation of the apparently boundless field of harmonic variation to a few types of chord.

Sauveur points out that every musical system is based on the division of the octave into constituent notes which sound agreeable to the ear, and are also practical for the playing of music. For European music he considers valid a natural diatonic system containing three elements:

8 : 9	9 : 10	15 : 16
c d	d e	e f
greater tone	lesser tone	semitone

Sauveur names three possible means of reproducing melody in the natural diatonic system:

(a) by means of instruments, whose tuning is effected exclusively by ear (e.g. the human voice or the violin family);

(b) by instruments whose notes are mechanically fixed by holes, keys, or frets, but on which a player with a sensitive ear can produce slight variations (e.g. wind instruments and viols);

(c) with keyed instruments, where the ear exerts no influence (organ, harpsichord, etc.).

The Foundations of Modern Music

Sauveur shows that even the ablest musicians cannot remain within the bounds of a purely diatonic system. They are forced to apply slight corrections to its intervals, if the song is to end in the key from which it started. These barely perceptible corrections are 'only possible because the ear remembers the sound of the keynote at the start, and alters the intervals to suit its purpose' (the fifth is the interval most frequently diminished).

No other acoustician brought so much interest to bear on the creative faculty of human auditory perception as Sauveur, who was himself totally debarred from its application. The clearer the scientific basis of sound became to him, the more his attention was directed towards the immeasurable psychophysiological factors in music.

The difficulties of applying a purely diatonic system made it necessary for Sauveur to establish a form of equal temperament. As in all his investigations, Sauveur aimed at creating an all-round system which should contain the best of all possible temperaments.

The mathematical precision with which he formulated his general system of temperament is still an example to us. The science of acoustics will have to bear Sauveur's experiments in mind, as the disruption of our equal-tempered scale, and the musical system on which it is based, becomes complete.

He suggests that only three systems approach the ideal, which he defines in the following terms: 'A tempered system should simplify the theoretical side of tonality. The octave should not be divided into too many notes, and the pure diatonic intervals should be altered as little as possible.'

The systems to be considered are those that temper in 31, in 43 and in 55 degrees.

The system of 31 degrees is the temperament of which Salinas and Mersenne had already disapproved and which Huyghens reintroduced in 1691 in 'Le Cycle Harmonique' (*Histoire des Ouvrages des Savants*).

Joseph Sauveur

According to Sauveur the system of temperament in 55 degrees was universally employed by musicians in 1700.

Finally temperament in 43 degrees was his own system of partition.

The system of twelve equally tempered notes, in use at the time, is commented on by Sauveur in the following words: 'This system is preferred by our less competent instrumentalists; it allows one to transpose easily without changing of interval. But more sensitive musicians have rejected it, because its intervals deviate from the natural diatonic norm.'

According to Sauveur, practical music teaches us that a system which tempers all intervals alike is less disturbing to the ear than one in which some intervals are markedly altered, while others remain purely diatonic. For instance, the larger intervals, represented by low proportions (e.g. the fifth, whose proportion is 2:3) react more sensitively to considerable alteration than the small intervals with correspondingly higher proportional values (e.g. the major third, 4:5).

Despite this new indication of the demands of the ear, Sauveur did not dare to put his discoveries and conclusions into practice. He did not propose the general introduction of an equal-tempered scale of twelve notes, as Werkmeister had done in 1691, and the Chinese musicologist Chu Tsai Yu a century earlier. The range of his experiments was both smaller and greater, for he wished to establish a system which should not only be the best, but should include all other systems.

5.

Table générale des Systèmes tempérés de Musique (1711)

The above *Mémoire* is the answer to a publication by Haefling, a musicologist from Anspach (*Miscellanea Berolinea*, 1710) who proposed a new temperament of 50 degrees. Sauveur countered with ill-concealed anger because this solution hindered his plan for putting acoustics and music on a generally interdependent level. Once more, he shows the necessity for a generally accepted division of the octave as a basic foundation, and returns to his division into 43 degrees, which was for him the most satisfactory and the only one capable of ascertaining the characteristic values of all other systems by means of heptameridians and decameridians.

Among modern musicologists, Hugo Riemann was particularly occupied with problems of musical temperament. An examination of the relevant articles in his *Musiklexikon* and *Handbuch der Musikwissenschaft* strengthens the impression that Riemann's ignorance of the meridian system does not affect the value of Sauveur's work, the full realization of which may perhaps be yet to come. In its place Riemann suggests two further temperaments, Mercator's old division of 53 degrees, and Janko's more recent plan of 41 degrees.

This *Mémoire* also throws an interesting light on the musical practices of the time. 'Neither nations nor even great composers can agree on the usage of augmented or diminished intervals. Their purpose is admittedly to make the music sound more piquant or sad; but agreement on this point has not helped our pundits to decide on the exact size of the intervals.'

Sauveur stands alone in his recognition, however indirect, of the aesthetic value of creative art. He is always aware of the creative powers at work in musical composition—powers which make applied acoustics one of the most delicate and scientifically complicated problems to be mastered.

Joseph Sauveur

6.

Rapport des Sons des Cordes d'Instruments de Musique, aux Flèches des Cordes; et nouvelle détermination des Sons fixes (1716).

Sauveur's last work on acoustics was completed in 1713, but it did not appear until after his death in 1716, when it formed part of Fontenelle's obituary notice.

Sauveur here returns to his original problem: that of fixing a standard pitch. Notwithstanding the ingenious indirect solution discovered in 1700, he continued to look for a new definition, which should be simpler in practice and more accurate in method. This he did by restricting himself to measuring strings, verifying the results by mathematical tests.

In this connection he makes a number of interesting observations, both physical and physiological, determining the maximum degree of tension for steel, iron and copper strings, as well as the faults due to the uneven quality of gut and silk strings.

He also proves that the ear is a more sensitive instrument than the eye, affirming that the ear can distinguish differences of a heptameridian (i.e. the 301st part of an octave).

He names sixteen cycles per second as the lowest, and 32,718 cycles per second as the highest limit of perception.

We also owe to him the following interesting remarks on the pitch of bells.

'The bells of *Notre-Dame de Paris* have names and pitches as follows:

Emanuel	*Marie*	*Gabrielle*	*Guillaume*	*Pasquier*	*Thibaut*	*Jean*
A	*B*	*C*	*D*	*E*	*F*	*G*

The bells in the two towers are: *Claude*   *Nicolas*

                                                          A   *B*

The Foundations of Modern Music

The bells in the little tower are:

Catherine	*Magdalaine*	*Mathphas*	*Barbe*	*Anne*
D	E		F	G

The bells of Saint Paul sound: **D** E F G A

Those of Saint Victor: D E F G A B

while the bells of Sainte Geneviève of Paris and of Saint Amé at Douay sound: D E F.'

In every case the scale of the bells is that of the Dorian tetrachord, whether it is only D E F G or whether it ascends as far as B and even D omitting C or, as in the bells of Notre-Dame, where it begins with the correspondingly lower tetrachord, A B C D.

Sauveur's collaborators were: M. Marius 'si connu par les Clavecins brisés et par ses autres inventions', Sieur Deslandes, and the famous Père Sébastien Truchet. He had worked with the latter between 1699 and 1700, and again in 1704. This led him to the modern view of the two opposing wave motions of a vibrating string, which combine to make one complete vibration.

Eventually he decided to standardize the pitch of a given note on a mathematical as well as a practical basis. Taking c' for his given note, at a frequency of 256 cycles per second, he reached it in all octaves by multiples of two: 2 4 8 16 32 64 128 256.

The *Mémoire* also contains a careful explanation of the relationship between organ foot-tone and pitch, according to which open organ-pipes with 2 foot tone gave c' at 256 cycles per second, with 4 foot 128 cycles per second and with 32 foot 16 cycles per second.

Joseph Sauveur

And here, for once, Sauveur draws conclusions outside the realms of music. He proves that, by exact determination of the pitch of bells, their relative and absolute weight may be deduced (cf. pitch examination in mine-shafts). By the same means it is possible to discover the rate of vibration of the vocal chords during singing, and of the lips when blowing instruments or whistling. All the natural frequencies of bodies sounding in resonance with them (e.g. sound-boards, vases and cavities in the human body), and even the scarcely perceptible micro-intervals of bird-song can equally be determined.

From this he deduces that a knowledge of the natural frequency of all terrestrial objects, and of all their mutations would facilitate an understanding of human nature and its changing conditions, including animals and all other earthly phenomena. If only antiquity had been able to fix the natural frequencies of things, we should know to-day what the men of those days were like, and what were the most important events in their lifetime.

FONTENELLE'S ACCOUNTS OF SAUVEUR
(1697—1733)

In 1697 Fontenelle was appointed permanent secretary to the *Académie des Sciences* at Paris. It was his duty to make annual reports on the publications of the academicians, and to write their obituary notices. From that date onwards he was the moving spirit of the Academy. His reports are perfect examples of popular scientific exposition. At the same time, they are remarkable for their fine literary style, superior intellectual qualities, and enthusiastic support of reason. The subjects follow one another naturally and the unimportant material is omitted. In this way Fontenelle throws new light on every discovery. The result of the two publications of the *Histoire de l'Académie des Sciences* is so important that one cannot discuss Sauveur's work without alluding to Fontenelle's reports.

The Foundations of Modern Music

The report of 1701 (*On a new system in Music*) makes it clear that Sauveur's investigation has an indirect bearing on the basis of musical composition. Fontenelle demands an aesthetic justification of Sauveur's theories. His remarks, frequently quoted, justify Fontenelle's claim to have penetrated the mysterious relationship between series of numbers and harmony of sound. He touches on the limits of aesthetic pleasure and also hints at their possible expansion. 'There is a limit to the many-sidedness of those perceptions which give pleasure to the soul. They should never be difficult to grasp, nor should they appear confused, or be composed of too many dissimilar ingredients.' Again he writes: 'Spiritual impressions which may in themselves be unpleasant, can be presented so many times in the company of pleasing elements, that the latter will be recalled with them, and they may thus by integration pass unnoticed.'

Fontenelle's aesthetic analysis soon led him to the problems of the ear. 'One note can easily arouse in the mind the idea of another, either its equal, (i.e. the unison) or one very similar (e.g. the octave). Both suggestions are so simple that the ear considers them as notes which it hears whether they have in fact been sounded or not. Fontenelle returns to this ability of the ear explaining the degrees of acceptability in the seconds (ratios of 8:9 and 9:10). For by frequently hearing the fifth and fourth (2:3 and 3:4) or the fourth and minor third (3:4 and 5:6) we notice the difference between these two corresponding types of seconds. The brain adds to its perception of the seconds something of the harmony of the greater intervals.

Fontenelle slowly inclines to make the ear the chief criterion, regardless of the numerical laws of musical intervals. In this way, the formation of the natural diatonic scale is explained by the necessity for a succession of notes in certain unequal proportions (8:9 / 9:10 / 15:16) which enable the most harmonious chords possible to be derived from the component notes (C:E / C:F / C:G, etc.).

He fully realizes the activity of aural perception in relation to

Joseph Sauveur

temperament, which means that the ear replaces the so-called natural sounds by a choice of notes better suited to its inward nature.

Fontenelle closes his report with this eulogy of Sauveur: 'All we need now is for musicians to hasten the introduction into music of this infinitely preferable tonal vocabulary.' Fontenelle's hope has not yet been fulfilled.

Musicians still prefer illogicalities hallowed by tradition to these modern improvements. Thus they still speak of whole-, semi-, and quarter-tones, as if these concepts signified different proportions of a tone, and not the distance between two sounds. They use a musical alphabet which jumps from A to H* and then returns to the usual letters C D E F. They complicate the octave divisions of sound with such names as subcontra-, contra-, Great, Little, 'one-dash' up to 'five-dash' octave, instead of signifying them simply from bottom to top by I, II, III, etc. They make horn players (as in 'horn in F' for example) transpose a fifth downwards in the treble clef, but force them to read a fourth up when they use the bass clef. Finally they allow the terms partial and overtone to denote the same thing, although the first partial should really stand for the fundamental itself, and the first overtone should signify the octave above that note.

The report of 1702 contains the passage, already quoted, about Sauveur, which made known his importance, both intellectually and musically:

This concept of the numerical proportions of notes is the representative expression of all the music that Nature has given us.

Music is thus a system of sound arising from harmonic notes. In other words, nature itself is the creator of art. That was Sauveur's great discovery, as Fontenelle saw it, and as indeed the next two centuries have proved it to be.

* Translator's note: This practice is confined to German-speaking countries.

The Foundations of Modern Music

This discovery is based on the known fact that over a long time artistic practice had unconsciously introduced a system which was yet far beyond the perception of its creators. Once more, the ear and its experience had caused practice to develop faster than theory.

But here the word *intuition* should be used rather than *experience*. Only a happy intuition could have led organ builders centuries before Sauveur to apply the unknown principle of harmonics to organ design.

Fontenelle's later reports show a marked decline in his interest in Sauveur. The reason is that the development of music had continued regardless of his system.

At the same time however, an unforeseen aspect of Sauveur's musical insight was recognized by Rameau. But by that time Fontenelle's understanding had ceased. This was also the reason why, at the end of his examination of Sauveur's last brilliant *Mémoire* of 1713, Fontenelle, astounded and shaken, asserts that 'in the hands of philosophers, music becomes merely the physics of sound' and why, after hearing examples of the pure music then coming to the fore (i.e. instrumental composition) he pronounced the famous words: 'Sonata' (that is to say 'absolute music') 'what do you want of me?'

RAMEAU'S EVALUATION OF SAUVEUR'S DISCOVERIES

'One experiment may easily lead to another.'

(Fontenelle).

Music makes nonsense of the stale proverb: 'There is nothing new under the sun.'

Polyphony and accompanied homophony belong exclusively to the western world. After a struggle lasting more than five hundred years polyphony attained its summit about 1550; while harmonically accompanied song did not arise until 1600. Bach and Handel used

Joseph Sauveur

both in a new means of expression which is found in the works of classical composers from 1780 onwards.

Sauveur, born deaf and dumb, stands at the entrance of this epoch. He provided the material for its development.

The pitch of any given note having been definitely fixed, it was no longer possible to transpose music as Bach often did. The transcription of his E major violin concerto into one in D for harpsichord would seem absurd to-day, and was then only aesthetically possible because pitch was not yet determined though the keys suited to each instrument were fixed by convention. At that time the harpsichord did not possess the e''', which occurs in the violin concerto; equally D major was, on grounds of temperament, a more suitable key for the harpsichord than the E major of the violin concerto.

Sauveur's determination of pitch made key a practical reality. J. S. Bach was one of the first to apply keys according to their fixed character. In 1725 he published the first part of *Das Wohltemperierte Klavier*, which goes twice through each of the major and minor keys.

To-day it is hard to imagine the momentous changes brought about by Sauveur's first discoveries in the field of acoustics. Music could at last sound as it was written: it could arouse the same emotions that had inspired it. It could at last really be (in sound) what it appeared to be (on paper).

But sound had first to be apprehended in its original form. Sauveur effected this by his principle of harmonics which unfolded the inner structure of music.

In his *Mémoire* of 1701, he first used the expression 'fundamental'.

In 1702 he made a calculation of all the consonant partials of the fundamental up to the 1,024th.

The actual sound is thus perceived as the sum of the fundamental and its corresponding overtones.

The Foundations of Modern Music

At the same time experience seemed to show that all resonant bodies obey the law of harmonics: the ear always appeared to hear the fifth and the third above (i.e. the third and fifth harmonics) as well as the fundamental.

The mathematical law, by which the vibration of the fundamental produces a series of sounds *ad infinitum*, fully corresponds to the acoustical combination of ascending real sounds forming a major chord.

It was then only a short step to Rameau's inspired conception of the chord as an aurally perceptible imitation of a natural phenomenon. (*Traité de l'Harmonie*, 1722).

Sauveur further pointed out the reciprocal powers of inverted intervals.

The harmonic series contains the notes of the major chord in its two possible inversions as well as in its root position:

C	g	e'		= Root position	$\frac{5}{3}$
1	3	5			
	g	e'	c''	= Second inversion	$\frac{6}{4}$
	3	5	8		
		e'	c''	g''	= First inversion	$\frac{6}{3}$
		5	8	12		

Thus the famous law of octave unisons made it possible to recognize these sequences also in the following arrangement:

g	c'	e'		= Second inversion	$\frac{6}{4}$
3	4	5			
	c'	e'	g'	= Root position	$\frac{5}{3}$
	4	5	6		
		e'	g'	c''	= First inversion	$\frac{6}{3}$
		5	6	8		

Joseph Sauveur

This facilitated Rameau's second discovery, which showed that reformation of the notes of a triad does not produce new and independent harmonies, but merely inversions of one and the same fundamental formation.

Sauveur and Rameau introduced the four following ideas into the theory of music:

the *fundamental*—as a tonic centre
the *major chord*—as a natural phenomenon
the *inversion*—as a variant of a chord
construction by thirds—as the law of chord formation.

Musicians could now establish the science of consonance and its correlations which henceforth, as 'harmony', was to dominate the whole art.

Rameau's concept of consecutive intervals in the harmonic series led him to the new and important idea that all melodic movement is the outcome of this harmonic foundation:

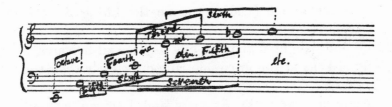

Sauveur's discoveries and Rameau's elaborations completely reversed the conception of music which had been current for more than a thousand years. It could now be affirmed that:

the fundamental supplies energy to all other notes;

basic harmony relates all other chords to itself;

single notes—the fixed points of polyphony—seem to give the impetus to a new kind of part-writing.

The Foundations of Modern Music

All tonal structure could now be explained as harmonic movement round a centre, which integrates even the most distant chordal formations and the furthest removed harmonies.

Physicists and mathematicians were brought into close contact with the new science of acoustics, which the *Académie des Sciences* had adopted in 1700 as an independent discipline. Thus De Mairan and De Gamaches gave their support in *Génération harmonique, ou traité de musique théorique et pratique* (Paris, Proult, 1737) to those extraordinary formulations in Rameau's *Génération harmonique* which deal with 'The fusion of commensurable vibratory waves in sound', and 'an analysis of the sounds produced by the vibrating fibres of the cochlea'.

The Academy expressed its public appreciation of Rameau's work in 1737 and 1749.

Sauveur died too early to receive the title of 'The Newton of Acoustics'. But his contemporaries soon named Rameau 'The Newton of Harmony'.

For the first time a musical reformer was also the theoretician of his own reforms.

From a hostile source (Diderot) came the biting remark about Rameau:

'His wife and daughter may die any day for all he cares, so long as the funeral bells at the graveside ring out clearly their third and fifth overtones.'

The revolution started by Sauveur and Rameau was as much comprehended by musicians as by theoreticians.

Certainly no other book on music has left such a deep and universal impression as Rameau's *Traité de l'Harmonie.* (*Traité de l'Harmonie, réduite à ses principes naturelles; divisé en 4 livres: I° Du rapport des raisons et proportions harmoniques. II° De la nature et de la propriété des accords et de tout ce qui peut servir à rendre une musique parfaite. III° Principes de composition. IV° Principes d'accompagnement.* (Paris, Ballard, 1722).

Joseph Sauveur

Handel gave his approval; Bach made certain reservations; Mattheson fought it with all his might; Sorge accepted the idea of a scientific theory of harmony; Marpurg introduced Rameau's ideas throughout Germany. For Sulzer's *Aesthetik der schönen Künste* (Aesthetics of Fine Art) they were a theoretical basis founded on Rousseau's *Dictionnaire de musique*. Marpurg's best pupil, Simon Sechter—with whom Schubert was planning to study counterpoint in 1827, a year before his death—continued to teach by Rameau's rules until 1850. And Anton Bruckner, a pupil of Sechter, took over from him Rameau's 'Manual of Thoroughbass' and his doctrine of chromatic chords derived from double roots.

Rameau's 'Construction of chords by thirds' is still in use to-day, and in spite of Hugo Riemann's bitter opposition it plays its part in almost all the experiments which touch on the nature of modern harmony.

II

The Secret of Creative Art

(Johann Sebastian Bach)

The Way to Bach
Rameau's Law of Artistic Expression
Bach and Rameau

The most important predecessors of Sauveur and Rameau were Francisco de Salinas (1513—1590) and Gioseffe Zarlino (1517—1590).

Salinas laid the foundations of acoustics by proving the law of octave unisons. Zarlino discovered the nature of harmony by recognizing the importance of the fifth consisting of two thirds. Salinas founded the purely diatonic system, while Zarlino was the first to contrast major (allegro—cheerful) with minor (mesto—sad) in church modes.

The predominance of three-part writing came to an end about 1550.

The tenor still provided the 'proper cadences' but no longer defined the key. The bass became the foundation of the music, retarded its movement, separated itself from the other voices and took over the final cadence.

The simultaneous setting of all the voices replaced the method of adding them one by one, while integrated harmony succeeded the old combination of intervals.

In 1594 the two great masters of counterpoint, Palestrina and Orlando di Lasso, died. With Jacopo Peri's *Dafne* (produced soon after) monody and the *basso continuo* came to take its place.

Johann Sebastian Bach

The vocal forms of this new art of accompanied monody were the opera, the oratorio and the cantata. Among its instrumental forms were the sonatas for solo instrument and continuo, for alternating ensembles of instruments, and for concertante instruments with accompanying parts.

The writing of a *basso continuo* enabled chords to be presented in a practical form.

In time the practice of indicating the tonic chord over a bass note ceased, while the figures 2 4 7 9 11 unmistakably marked the characteristic dissonances. Strict conventions were employed for chords over single notes of the scale, and these gave rise to the *Regola dell'-ottava* of the Italian masters.

The year 1700 saw the foundation of acoustical science. In 1750, Johann Sebastian Bach died. While the principles of basso continuo were moving to their climax, the work of Sauveur and Rameau began to revolutionize music.

'To experience music fully is to yield to the principle through which music affects us. Now this principle is Nature.'   (Rameau, 1754).

The decisive musical discovery of the eighteenth century was Sauveur's proof of the natural structure of musical sound. His conception of a fundamental and its overtones suggested the following ideas to the theory of music.

1. Every musical sound is the fundamental of a series of overtones and as such carries its own harmony of a major triad (the tonic).

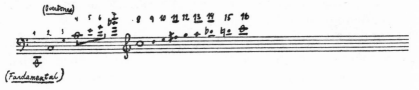

The Secret of Creative Art

2. The series of overtones includes almost all notes and therefore almost all intervals.

3. The fundamental is the note that occurs most frequently in the series of overtones (1/2/4/8/16).

4. Every series of overtones contains the inversions as well as the root position of the major triad from its fundamental (3/4/5 and 5/6/8).

5. A second natural major triad is based on the fifth above the fundamental (dominant triad).

6. Every major triad thus appears in a second series of overtones as the chord on the fifth degree.

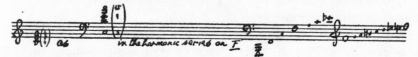

7. The fundamental common chord has thus three basic uses: as tonic, as dominant (the fifth above), and as subdominant harmony (the fifth below).

8. Musical sound *per se* tends to modulate.

Rameau found in these facts the objective structure of music, which revealed itself independently of the personal whim of composers, performers or audience. With the intuition of the creative artist he used these facts in two treatises to develop the laws of musical expression based on harmony. (*Observation sur notre instinct pour la musique, 1754. Code de musique pratique, 1760.*)

The following statement was made by Rameau in answer to J. J. Rousseau's *Critique* of the famous monologue in Lully's *Armide*:

'Monotony can be defined as the consequence of an unrealized tendency to progress by modulation:

'Music for trumpet and natural horn, which can only modulate into the dominant, is emotionally effective only when varied in tempo and rhythm.'

The following passages exemplify the feeling of expressive ascent in modulation to the dominant, and the depressing effect of progression into the subdominant:

'Do we not suffer the same feeling of oppression as the heroine herself, when the melody drops from c' to f' at the words *tristes apprêts?*

If the f' were replaced by a g' and the harmony left unchanged, the emotions would not be aroused. A more lively rhythm and fresh words of a cheerful character might make the passage effective.'

'Again at the whispered words: 'Si quelqu'un le peut être' Lully modulates into the subdominant, instead of remaining in the tonic. Sensitivity led him to make this change which enables the listener to realize the emotional state of the singer:

At the words which follow Armide's cry 'Le vainqueur de Renaud' the music seems to express humiliation and fear that she may fail to triumph over the hero.

Had Lully merely intended to describe the courage of the hero, without Armide's dread of defeat, he would certainly have contrived such an harmonic progression as this:

If these passages are both sung without the text, but with appropriate tempi, the differing emotions become apparent. It will be observed that the modulating fall from f' sharp to f' natural softens the texture, while the modulation to the dominant (through c' sharp instead of c') causes one to sing more vigorously, and to bring to the passage the desired effect of pride.'

Apart from musical monotony the above examples deal with the effects of dominant and subdominant modulation, while those that follow are concerned with the contrast between major and minor.

'The monologue 'Enfin il est dans ma puissance' begins in E minor:

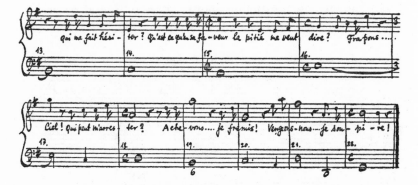

In order to lend more force to Armide's description of the hero, the g' sharp of the subdominant (A minor) suggests her reflective words: 'Le charme du sommeil le livre à ma vengeance. The outcry 'Je vais percer son invincible coeur' returns once more to E minor.

Had Lully remained in G major at the words 'le charme du sommeil le livre à ma vengeance' the musical effect and the words would contradict each other.

The forceful effect of G major in 'Ce superbe vainqueur' is doubled by the contrast with the gentle E minor tonality at the beginning.

The G sharp in the bass implies the subdominant A minor. But Lully goes directly into the dominant of E minor. This strengthens the power of the words 'le livre à ma vengeance' (bars 5 and 6).

The voice here drops, in order to flare up again at the cry,

The Secret of Creative Art

'Je vais percer son invincible coeur' (bars 6, 7 and 8) and so to reveal all the rage with which Armide is filled.'

This example shows Lully's continuation of Armide's monologue and Rameau's harmonic elaborations. They exemplify the following principle: 'more than just eyesight is needed to see and bring out the raising and lowering of pitch (♯, ♮ and ♭) which are neither indicated in the melody and the bass, nor in the figuring, and which are indeed hidden in Lully's original text.'

Johann Sebastian Bach

The explanation in Rameau's analysis of the harmonic progression in Lully's monologue formed the basis of his book *On the sensible use of modulation to develop the law of musical expression*.

In it he says: 'all tonalities moving in the direction of the dominant express warmth, light and cheerfulness; while those moving towards the subdominant give the effect of cold, darkness and despair.'

'Harmony alone can rouse the passions. Melody saps them of their vitality.'   (Rameau, 1754).

How is it possible for one and the same chorale tune to express two fundamentally different feelings, in such a way that one version sounds secular and the other fades away like a funeral dirge?

Bach was thirty-five when in 1720 he copied this chorale into the organ book of his first wife:

Wenn wir in höchsten Nöten sein
und wissen nicht, wo aus noch ein,
und finden weder Hülf noch Rat,
ob wir gleich sorgen früh und spat:
so ist dies unser Trost allein,
dass wir zusammen allgemein
dich anrufen, o treuer Gott,
um Rettung aus der Angst und Not.

[Whene'er we faint with deep distress
And know no ease from wretchedness:
When none will help us in our plight,
Weeping alike by day and night,
This is our only comfort then,
To join with all our fellowmen
In calling on Thee, Lord most dear,
To save us from distress and fear.]

63

Thirty years later, blind and overshadowed by death, he dictated a chorale prelude on the same melody.

> Vor deinen Thron tret' ich hiermit,
> o Gott und dich demütig bitt:
> wend' dein genädig Angesicht
> von mir betrübtem Sünder nicht.

> [Before Thy Throne, O God, I stand
> And humbly pray with outstretched hand
> Turn not Thy face away from me,
> Most wretched sinner though I be.]

Johann Sebastian Bach

In the chorale of 1720 the phrases of the melody follow one another directly. The pauses are merely breaks, necessary in congregational singing, after which the hymn continues without further delay.

In the first strain of the organ prelude of 1750, the *canto fermo* is ornamented according to traditional practice while the second is true to the original; both the third and fourth introduce one passing-note. Long cadences replace the pauses.

The note against note harmonization of the chorale is slackened to give a polyphonic effect, by means of thematic imitation, suspensions, passing-notes and the *nota cambiata.*

The imitative parts of the chorale prelude blend together in chordal harmony and suggest the joint meditation of a community.

In the earlier setting each line of the chorale begins diatonically; in the prelude for organ the entries are masked by evasive harmonies.

The clear light which the tonic and dominant relationship gives is prevalent in the chorale.

Secondary chords cast a shade of twilight on the chorale prelude.

The relative minor is used in the chorale to supply lively contrast, but in the organ version it transforms the warm light of G major into the tender sadness of the minor key.

The Secret of Creative Art

Whereas the cadences of the chorale are unmistakably clear, in the chorale prelude inverted imitations and interrupted cadences transform the end of each line into a calm succession of plagal harmonies broadly woven round the melody.

These expressive devices are carried out without any melodic change, and the polyphonic structure of the chorale prelude gives the impression of a profound meditation on the simple harmonic setting of the chorale version.

The new aspect is, however, due to the changed harmonic scheme. The melody seems in the chorale prelude to have assumed a more spiritual and profound mode of expression.

All Rameau's ideas on dominant and subdominant tonalities and their different powers of expression, like those on the contrasted characters of major and minor, seem to have been prompted by Bach's last composition.

The theories of the French and the practical work of the German composer are thus connected. They found an objective criterion for an art that was greater than its creators, that liberated some of the technique of artistic expression from arbitrary judgment, and seemed to subordinate them to exclusively musical laws.

THE CREATIVE PROCESS IN ART

Creation is a purely auto-repetitive process: all living things reproduce themselves in a ceaseless but vain attempt to check the flow of time.

Man alone does not merely repeat himself: in his art he creates a prototype reflecting an order higher than the unreasoning existence of nature.

I

In 1788, in less than three months, Mozart composed his last three symphonies: the E♭, the tragic G minor and the triumphant 'Jupiter' in C major.

The Creative Process in Art

Mozart's outward existence was at that time a negative one. All hope of self-respecting employment had faded. Financial worries could no longer be relieved by loans. His wife was in a constant state of ill-health, he himself physically exhausted. The heartfelt intimacy with his father in his youth was now a thing of the past.

Mozart now had to give music lessons to eke out a miserable existence. He had to write begging letters, the bitterness of which is painful to read. Surely the last three symphonies should reflect his rank poverty, unrest and humiliation. A short while before, he had written to his father the remarkable letter in which he told him that his heart had been free from fear since he began thinking every day about death, and that nothing could affect or worry him any more. His lofty resignation should surely break through the last three symphonies.

And should not the reflection of life's crushing blows, the brief joys and lasting sorrows of each day, find a place in his works? Had it happened so, they would not be able to take the listener out of himself by the sheer power of their unforgettable brilliance.

The content of a work of art consists in the exposition of higher forms which strike humanity by their glorious and radiant light.

The finished composition is not an end but a beginning. It opens up possibilities of finer things, shows us profounder realities and makes us realize our true nature.

'All men shall be brothers!' During his life the lonely and desolate Beethoven could only enter the temple of Apollo as a 'brother in spirit'. Nevertheless in revealing the burning passion of Schiller's words, the Ninth Symphony could conquer the bitterness of misanthropy and eliminate hardheartedness.

Knowledge and experience have transformed the triumphant call 'All men shall be brothers' into the doubt 'Can all men be brothers?' The solo quartet dies away in sorrow sweeter than has yet been heard by men. The brightness of the B major section turns despondently into the minor key at the end of the adagio . . .

But creative art goes farther for it conquers doubt through knowledge. Neither delusion nor illusion makes the chorus exclaim 'Seid umschlungen Millionen, diesen Kuss der ganzen Welt!' The absolute truth of creative imagination reaches above our limited perception, offering to the doubtful and the weary eternal certainty.

A work of art is a manifesto, unquestioning and fearless. It is a sensory experience, an appeal to the spirit not to be resisted.

II

Soul, spirit and body move in concord at the sound of music.

No dramatic expression, no sculptured gesture in its immobility, no cry of despair, however real, so directly touches the centre of the nervous system as the power of the human voice.

A quiver runs through us when Caruso sings a top B flat even on a gramophone record. This applies equally to a light popular song or the most exquisite work. The music makes us move to the rhythm.

The distant 'tantantara tsing boom' of a military band is enough to affect everybody by its electrifying rhythm. Children hop downstairs in time to it, the feet of the reader tap in rhythm, people in the street walk in step to it. They are bound by one force that sets their bodies in motion.

When the first instrument begins the six-voice ricercare from Bach's *Musical Offering* all chance solutions are silenced and we become conscious of a logic that must in the end be accepted as unquestionable.

Gräser's edition of Bach's *Art of Fugue* was used for its first performance at the Salle Pleyel in Paris in 1928. On this occasion, an incident memorably showed music's power to lay bare a listener's personality. The orchestra reached the close of the four part mirror fugue No. XVIII. As the last chords died away, a solitary voice was heard pealing, high above, the theme of the fugue to come. Then it too was silent and like a faint echo, a voice from the far end of the concert hall, answered with a soft 'bravo'.

Never was I more aware of the consonance of musical material and human personality than in this subconscious reply of a single voice to a single note. The mere note persisted as a gentle vibration of the musical element uniting mind and soul.

III

Music is enchantment perceived by the ear; it can unite men's intellects and lift the mind to higher spheres of thought.

In a perfect work of art these attributes are in harmony.

Beauty in music derives from the quality of its material, from melody, harmony, rhythm and tone colour.

The borderline of vulgarity begins when the purely sensuous material cannot be transformed into a superior type of art.

Gounod's *Ave Maria* is anything but an ill-constructed melody. On the contrary, analysis would prove its profound effect on an everyday audience. Nevertheless it is almost banal, for its effect is the result of a musical intoxication that contradicts the austere harmony of Bach.

Rhythm moulds men's hearts into a larger unity. Johann Strauss' *Blue Danube* Waltz makes our hearts beat in unison today as it did a hundred years ago. No one can remain outside its all-embracing spell. The wooing regularity of the rhythm and the enchanting melody above it create an atmosphere of tenderness and strength which makes the self recede only to become part of a new and harmonious whole.

The theme of the *Art of Fugue* undergoes the following trans-formations:

Each of these variants not only gives rise to a fresh musical form but it also evokes a different reaction in the audience.

Inversion of the theme reverses the subject's effect: tension becomes relaxation and determination indecision (example 1).

Diminution and augmentation provide the theme with a new tempo and a different mood, in such a way that the same melody inspires the listener with fresh vigour (examples 2 and 3).

Rhythmic changes are intentional. In spite of the quadruple difference in time, examples 2 and 3 produce the same effect by use of a similar rhythmic figure.

The Creative Process in Art

In example 4 the rests are so grouped as to maintain a feeling of unswerving resolve.

The use of syncopation in example 5 leaves the theme in a state of suspense, while in example 6 it is in apparent meditation. Example 7 converts this tendency into almost painfully vehement obstinacy.

The hidden syncopations in example 8, sometimes combined with passing notes, give fresh vitality to the movement by interrupting the flow of thought.

Metrical changes affect the character of the piece. The 3/4 time-signature of example 9 transforms the placid subject into a gay gigue, while the 3/2 metre of example 6 lends it the melancholy character of a sarabande.

The change from minor to major in example 10 turns tension into relaxation. In example 11, the sixth in the melody becomes a seventh and imparts expanding force to the familiar theme.

In example 12 the free use of passing- and changing-notes gives an almost independent character to the melody. It is the only example where intervals are changed to any marked degree; for instance, in the last bar, the g is altogether absent and the compass of the theme, as exposed so far (a seventh in example 11), is increased to the ninth (A-B flat).

All these melodic transformations affect the audience appreciably on hearing the work.

Yet it is not essential for the intellect to apprehend these changes. They are experienced however much they may be resisted. The work becomes part of our lives; it dwells in us, until its perfection outshines the weakness of our nature.

A work of art is not only an objective cultural experience, the perception and study of which proves satisfying; it also has a subjective force, active and formative in its penetrating power.

Two of its effects are significant. Art enables man to practise facul-

71

The Secret of Creative Art

ties which he has not hitherto been able to develop. Through art he also experiences a degree of communal feeling which society has not yet been able to realize.

IV

Physiology and psychology alike teach us that man is incapable of absorbing several impressions at once.

He cannot simultaneously appreciate to the full several different sensations or intellectual ideas. He cannot, for instance, clearly distinguish the constituent sounds in a complicated chord. He cannot separate the rhythmic germs that are combined in polyrhythmic, or the various melodic lines that are woven together in polyphonic, passages.

But the richest polyphonic texture, the most diversely organized rhythmic features, the most complicated harmonic progressions can reach their audience, and make a deep impression by coming to life in the listener.

The double fugue at the end of Beethoven's Ninth Symphony combines the gigue-like strains of 'Freude, schöner Götterfunken' with the solemn strides of 'Seid umschlungen, Millionen'.

An audience is no more able to appreciate each of the two simultaneous melodic lines than to think of the two ideas at once. But whereas the verbal ideas, simultaneously expressed, destroy and nullify each other's significance, the simultaneous melodies can penetrate the intellect through their sensuous intensity.

Music is thus seen to have practical powers beyond the scope of human comprehension. It can induce a simultaneous perception and experience of several different values:

The Creative Process in Art

In bars 5 to 8 of the first fugue from the *Art of Fugue*, the subject and its counterpoint are combined in contrast. The tonal answer in the soprano weakens the fifth of the theme by making it a fourth. The alto becomes an independent countersubject in bar 6, due to the harmonic fall in the soprano voice, and this in its turn is diminished by the new impetus of the theme, in bars 7 and 8, returning to the diatonic e' f♯' g':

Two totally different expressions of energy are presented in the two voices which, while equally influencing each other, exert different qualities of emotion that can be felt simultaneously.

The multiple rhythms in the example below occur in the Eroica Symphony. In listening the ear cannot analyse the contrasted elements, though it can certainly appreciate them.

It will thus be seen that musical appreciation provides abilities far in advance of human organic development.

Music allows us to exert faculties which anticipate future generations. Once more, the old saying 'There is nothing new under the sun' has been proved wrong. It has too often been used to discredit the limitless quest of the creative spirit.

73

The Secret of Creative Art

The perfection of polyphonic art was the perfection of a social ideal. A more valuable example than that presented in the six-voice ricercare from Bach's *Musical Offering* could not be imagined.

When man is alone, terror of the infinite takes hold of him. Mystery surrounds him everywhere, and he is thrown back on reality. Given a companion, some of the mysteries can be explained. A third person, however, seems only to turn the truths to truisms. As the number increases the standard is lowered, and collectivity seems to bring with it the dissolution of superior individual powers.

But what is the result of collectivity in art, as in Bach's six-voice ricercare? As the number increases standards are raised and the whole unites all that is finest in each part. The separate elements reveal a two-fold nature, that of effective subject and responsive object. Each voice is at the same time a subject and a countersubject, a thought and the result of that thought.

Order and courtesy are the foundations of polyphony. He who is called to speak hears also what the others are saying.

'Six heads are better than one!'

Team-work gives the individual the richest opportunity for display. The old proverb teaches us the significance of polyphony. It is no vague doctrine, but a manifestation in artistic terms of innate but as yet impracticable human faculties.

THE PERFECT WORK OF ART

> 'Genius is 1 per cent inspiration, and 99 per cent perspiration.' (Edison).

Almost all creative artists have laid less stress on inspiration than on the perfection of technique.

A work of art is without prototype, an achievement that transcends its creator. In it the artist attempts to bring more refined orders of existence into being. If this be true, there is no doubt that only an exceptional ability and an infinite capacity for taking pains can ultimately achieve perfection.

This attitude was held by Bach as well as by Goethe. Mozart bore witness to it in the dedication of his quartets (1785). It underlies the famous saying of Haydn in his old age: 'Now that I no longer write symphonies, I know at last how to write for woodwind.' Beethoven finally proves it by his numerous alterations to the 'Joy-motive'.

Is creation perfected consciously or unconsciously? Is it brought about by musical material, or by intellectual faculties? And which of these formed the basis of that most perfect of all works, Bach's chorale prelude on 'Vor Deinen Thron tret' ich hiermit'?

Art can only be creative by a delicate interplay of consciousness and intuition. Even when consciousness appears to predominate, intuitive sensibility prevents it from assuming a cerebral character. Even the trance-like creative processes must contain an element of the reflecting consciousness. In this way a well constructed artistic organism is created.

I

If creative inspiration ever guided a man, that man was Schubert, when he wrote his Unfinished Symphony. Nevertheless artistic consciousness is everywhere perceptible in its most alert form. An example of this occurs when the nine bar violoncello tune, which forms the second subject, is repeated by the violins, and then, instead of returning to the tonic G major, is lost in the general pause:

The Secret of Creative Art

The tragic tension of this passage is due first to the silence that replaces the missing chord of G major and then to the music which attempts successive resolutions into C minor (subdominant), G minor and E flat (submediant).

Schubert's audacity, in interrupting the expected cadence in G major with these unexpected chords, argues a creative intellect of the utmost alertness.

Nevertheless Schubert remains the great Master of the subconscious in music. This rhapsodic, almost improvisatory quality of his music can be sensed even in his most logically constructed compositions. It is as if the work only came into being at the moment of performance. Such is the cogent effect of the Unfinished Symphony.

Beethoven's powerful transformation of the theme of the last movement of Mozart's G minor symphony into the theme of the Scherzo of his own fifth symphony:

may well be compared with Schubert's improvisation on it at the beginning of the Unfinished Symphony.

The comparison clearly demonstrates how differently the minds of these two composers worked. But Schubert had the highest opinion of

The Perfect Work of Art

Beethoven's inspiration, as the following words show: 'In Beethoven, art has become science: he knows his powers, and phantasy obeys his profound inspiration.'

'He can do everything, but we are still unable to understand all that he does.' Schubert's last remark about Beethoven could equally well apply to the composer of the Unfinished Symphony. For in both movements of this symphony, dream-like inspiration and awareness stand side by side.

The two thematic motives, quoted above, which start the Unfinished:

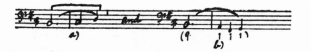

twice move away from the same note towards the nearest third, and both permeate and lend impetus to the whole work.

The melodic motive (a) impregnates the accompanying figure of the first subject, while a diminished version of (b) provides a tireless rhythmic bass.

Both motives are found together in bars two and four of the melody:

The symmetry of bars five to seven of this melody is determined by motive (a):

The Secret of Creative Art

The second subject uses the two motives for an identical effect:

The combination of the two motives in bar three of the above governs the dialogue-like treatment of the second subject as below:

The development section is derived from the two motives. It begins with treatment of (a) in imitation and so intensification.

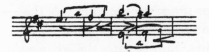

This is combined with its own inversion and the whole structure broadens out over a dominant minor ninth:

At the climax of the development, the two motives alternately dominate the music:

and motive (a) eventually remains alone, first in an altered form of its inversion:

then in its straightforward inverted form:

lastly in a diminished version of its accompanying form:

Just before the recapitulation, both motives are brought together again.

The Coda is supplied by the motives in their original form.

The Unfinished thus demonstrates a new method of thematic treatment; all its main features derive from one basic idea. This idea is heard at the start of the development section, introduces its climax and begins the Coda.

Only the rhythmic unity of the first movement of Beethoven's fifth symphony can be compared with Schubert's concentration of melodic material in this movement; but the two compositions draw on different intellectual processes. Beethoven's treatment grows out of an act of volition, Schubert's from the presentiment of an emotional impression.

The Secret of Creative Art

The magic in Schubert's music that seems to spring from the subconscious is shown by the apparent lack of necessity for completing the Unfinished Symphony. It is evident too at the beginning of its second movement, which induces the most deeply satisfying release from tension that music has ever known.

The chief key centres of the first movement are related by the notes of a descending minor triad: B minor (first subject), G major (second subject), E minor (development). But the second movement is in E major. This tonality is prepared by the long development section of the first movement in E minor. Its broadening-out into E major has the same uplifting effect as the transformation into the major of motive (a), which also dominates the second movement, and the simultaneous interlacing of both halves of motive (b):

Here again it is unimportant that the listener should be aware of the hidden details. A sensitive appreciation of Schubert's emotional background will enable him unconsciously to realize the power of this work's thematic structure.

II

The subject of the *Art of Fugue* is equally an inspiration. But at the same time it must have been conceived with the greatest deliberation.

The Perfect Work of Art

It contains both types of melodic formation. The first phrase is formed by the notes of the tonic chord and is followed by a melodic line made up of passing- and changing-notes. The whole has the effect of a paraphrase on a pedal-point D heard in the subconscious mind.

The melodic implications of this theme are far-reaching, including both the inverted and cancrizan forms of the theme.

Creative consciousness and intuition are here so singularly interwoven that it is difficult to say which is the more important.

More wonderful still than the development of the *Art of Fugue* from a single germ is the introduction and gradual development of the B - A - C - H* theme:

1 2 3 4

This chromatic figure makes its first appearance in the third fugue, at bar 5, in a form as yet unclarified:

Its first regular entry occurs three bars from the end of the fourth fugue, so skilfully worked into the musical texture that only a very acute ear can recognize it as the first foreshadowing of the B-A-C-H motive:

* Translator's note: In German speaking countries B is the name for B♭ and H for B♮.

At the beginning of the triple fugue (No. VIII) the chromatic motive B - A - C - H reappears in its unresolved form:

Here, however, it has become the core of the first of nine themes which Bach, in the course of the *Art of Fugue*, develops side by side with the principal theme:

The nine new themes are:

Nos. 1 and 2 in the triple fugue (No. VIII).

No. 3 in the double fugue (No. IX).

No. 4 in the double fugue (No. X).

No. 5 and 6 in the triple fugue (No. XI).

Nos. 7, 8 and 9 in the uncompleted fugue with four subjects (No. XIX).

The last of these themes introduces—for the first and only time in his life—Bach's own name.

The eleventh fugue which has three subjects is an inversion of No. VIII. Here the weary fall of the theme C-H-B-A is transformed into the passionate surging movement of:

The Perfect Work of Art

In Nos. VIII and XI alike, the B-A-C-H theme strives for a shape, though it can only develop other melodies; it is felt in the second of the new themes and dominates the double fugue:

But it is also present in the second of these two themes in a diminished form which can only be recognized if written in reverse:

The motive is developed three times in this fugue:

(a) 1 2 3 and (b) 7 6 5

3 4 5   5 4 3

5 6 7   3 2 1

In this way the B-A-C-H theme appears transposed a fifth higher, as (a) 4 5 6 7:

It is still in its anagrammatic form. But if (a) 4 5 6 7 is turned round, it becomes (b) 7 6 5 4:

In this way the B-A-C-H theme is found to be the secret driving-force behind the double fugue's second subject.

The Secret of Creative Art

The eleventh fugue in three parts inverts No. VIII, thus making clearly recognizable the B-A-C-H material when the two themes are combined as a double fugue:

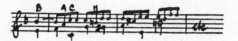

In contrapunctus XV, the B-A-C-H material at last succeeds in penetrating the main subject of the work, and thereby infuses its transcendent tranquillity with an emotion that comes near to passion:

It is to be found in the second bar which, transposed up a fifth, reads:

All these attempts to discourage his own presumption are ended in the second and final entry of the B-A-C-H theme in the last fugue. Its form is the same as in the 'inaudible' entry at the end of the fourth fugue. Bach's secret, there consciously withheld, is here announced to all ears.

The Perfect Work of Art

III

How could Beethoven set Schiller's impassioned hymn 'Freude, schöner Götterfunken, Tochter aus Elysium' to a tune so completely different in character?

When the theme is first announced by the solo bass, and later by the chorus in unison, its strutting crotchets have more the character of a cheerful carol than of an exultant shout.

And how could Beethoven set the text so waywardly as to neglect Schiller's verbal rhythms and the poem's sparkling tempo?

Was it consciously, just as Bach used a neutral basic form to construct the main theme of the *Art of Fugue*? Beethoven employed a basic melody as a foundation for free variations; it forms the core of the development and its climax and permeates the ecstasy of the finale.

Construction and progressive analysis of the Joy theme in the finale of Beethoven's Ninth Symphony.

The Secret of Creative Art

I. *Instrumental Exposition.*

II. *Variations.*

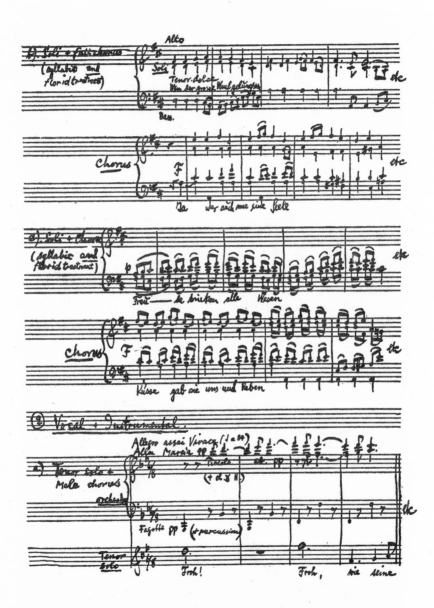

87

IV

However there are compositions which seem to have been inspired by their own medium. As an example let us cite Maurice Ravel's Introduction and Allegro for solo harp, flute, clarinet and string quartet, published in 1906.

The Secret of Creative Art

The fresh rhapsodic character of this work is derived from the surging, exuberant timbre of the harp. The instrument's abundant richness in delicate sounds inspired the structure and episodes of the piece.

The harp's particular technical potentialities also influenced Ravel's melodic idiom, choice of harmonies, and instrumental treatment. The medium which inspired him provided an incentive to create new modes of expression, and led Ravel's imagination to find an ethereal shimmering texture never before realized in music.

The harp's particular technical features comprise:

(a) the arpeggio, through a compass of almost six octaves.
(b) the glissando, through the same range, and with the instrument tuned to a single chord.
(c) the bisbigliando, i.e. repetition of the same note on two different strings.
(d) use of the harmonics, either singly or on several different notes.

The characteristics peculiar to the harp are:

(e) its facility for changing the tuning of many chords and sequences of notes.
(f) the effect of the pedals which, unlike the piano whose pedal-action merges single notes, increases the delicacy of the instrument's natural sound.
(g) the wonderful richness of its timbre and expressive power, which allows it to sound at any time either full or thin, muted or brilliant.

These technical effects and characteristics of the harp form the basis of Ravel's Introduction and Allegro. An element of improvisation is used to deepen the imaginative character of this work of genius.

A solo cadenza is built into the Allegro and here the harp is used as Ravel's intuition understood it. The atmosphere here is of spiritual melancholy, of mounting passion concealed by sweetness. There is an intimate ethereal quality about it, anxious but delicately expressive.

90

The Perfect Work of Art

All this is derived—with exquisite imaginative mastery—from the harp's natural sound. It characterizes the whole work and is evident in the Introduction from the sweeping harp chords and the silvery tones of wind and strings that precede it.

It is reflected in the adaptation of classical form to which it adds an unexpectedly new range.

The cadenza, which is really the beginning of the recapitulation, contains both themes of the Introduction. It condenses the melodic line and carries it away into the sublime realms of the abstract.

Both themes of the Allegro (in sonata form) derive from the Introduction. In spite of its apparent lack of structural tautness it has a strictly classical unity.

Each of the marked passages—both parts of the Introduction (IIa and IIb); the exposition (III) and the development section (IV) of the allegro; the recapitulation in the cadenza, the second allegro, and the coda (V)—demonstrates a different technical quality of the harp.

Ravel's work demonstrates to perfection the power of music to draw inspiration from its own material medium.

BACH'S LAST COMPOSITION

Bach's Last Composition

The Secret of Creative Art

The secret of artistic creation was never more evident than in the so-called final chorale of the *Art of Fugue*.

Bach, a blind man on his deathbed, dictated this masterwork to his son-in-law Altnikol. Beauty, power and imagination, the ideal components of a perfect work of art, are here abundantly present. The euphony of the four-part movement is awe-inspiring. Whenever the chorale enters one feels illuminated; the flow and structure of the work release an impression of unattainable freedom.

Whether this chorale prelude is played on the organ, by a string quartet or by four wind instruments, its magic is unimpaired: such pure music is self-expressive. A similar effect is felt in the *Ave Maria* from Verdi's *Quattro Pezzi Sacri*, written on a *scala enigmatica* 150 years after Bach's death.

For Bach's contemporaries, the chorale tune illustrated the text and mood of the hymn. The composer had at his disposal symbols familiar to his audience. Whether he used a song of praise, or of mourning, or of defiance, the congregation was in accord with the feeling of the words. As a result, the composer could, without fear of being misunderstood, allow personal phantasy to transform the music.

The chorale prelude is like a sermon; meditations on each strain follow in turn, until the whole melody has been used as a *Canto Fermo*. No technique could serve this purpose better than imitative counterpoint.

'Before thy throne, O God I stand', reads the text with which the tenor begins the tune. It transports the listener at once into the mood of the funeral hymn, the last line of which is the petition 'Grant to me, Lord, a blessed end'.

What a blessing it is to be universally understood! How the audience and the emotional background are helped by knowing the words of the chorale! Thus the chorale prelude can make use of the most subtle intellectual ideas without confusing the listener. Intellect and emotions work together and the moving beauty of this four-part movement penetrates all hearts.

Bach's Last Composition

The structure of the work is easily perceived if it is performed by a carefully chosen mixed choir, who should for preference sing pianissimo throughout, *mezza voce* and with closed lips. No nuances are necessary, nor any prepared phrasing. The texture of the voices sinks and merges dreamlike in its own purity. Goethe said in 1827 after listening to Bach's music: 'One seems neither to possess nor to need one's ears; still less eyes or any other sense.' . . .

The tempo is particularly significant, for the limit of its speed is fixed by the problem of making intelligible the unity of the melody.

Two considerations regulate the tempo:

(a) the diminished version of the chorale theme with which the tenor begins:

(b) its corresponding entry in the chorale:

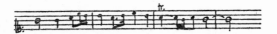

The metronome marking which suits both forms of the melody is: ♪=72 (Mälzel's metronome).

This allows the listener to think in terms of two quavers together, and to perceive the tenor theme of a bar and a half as a whole; in addition it prevents the *Canto Fermo* from being broken up into disconnected single notes.

This tempo, which has been arrived at by theoretical and practical experience, corresponds to the *Integer Valor* of the Middle Ages, and is the human normal value, by which seventy-two pulse beats and eighteen full respirations are produced every minute. This means that each 8/8 bar of the chorale prelude corresponds to one deep inhalation and expiration (at about the rate produced in deep sleep). This total relaxation of the physique corresponds also with the physical fatigue of the blind and dying Bach. Suddenly and almost physically one understands how this ethereal chorale prelude came to be composed over the hymn tune, and how the final brightness of a body about to return to nature could become reflected in its structure.

I

Beauties of sonority in the chorale prelude.

The secret of the euphonious character of Bach's music lies in the fact that its compass was naturally limited by that of the human voice. The upper voice rarely rises above g'' at the top of the treble stave, nor does the bass move below the singer's low E. This means that within this limited compass, four voices merge naturally into one another. Bach's polyphony contains no gaps, and those that do occur are definitely intended.

The shortened versions of the melody are significant:

Each of the four tenor phrases is diatonic and symmetrically constructed. There is only one interpolated third, in the third phrase, at bar 23.

The first and last phrases limit themselves to the compass of a fourth. The lively second phrase embraces a fifth, while the expressive third enlarges this to an octave.

Bach's Last Composition

The diminished forms of the phrases transform the lengthy divisions of the chorale into easily appreciated melodic groups. This gives a simple and natural impression and enables performers and audience alike to concentrate on the problems of sound.

The individual treatment of the four voices makes listening almost effortless. This is brought about

(1) by corresponding melodic and rhythmic treatment:

(2) by use of complementary rhythms:

(3) by treating the themes in contrary motion:

(4) by using diminution of the themes in stretto:

(5) by varying the direction of movement:

(6) by interlocking diminutions:

(7) by use of parallel movement at cadences:

In all these places (and many others) auditory and psychological processes make for easier comprehension. Satisfaction ensues from an effortless grasp of complex movement and results in a feeling of vivid sensory pleasure.

Bach's Last Composition

II

Bach's technique of expression.

(a) The expressive medium of imitative music.

The imitative repetition of a theme on another degree of the scale has an effect similar to that experienced when, on a walk that one knows well, one suddenly finds oneself crossing a parallel path, either higher or lower than the accustomed one, of a different breadth and with a different kind of surface. The walker immediately loses all sense of direction:

Diminution and augmentation of a theme induce a feeling similar to that experienced by one who, accustomed to travelling over a certain road every day at a certain pace, has suddenly to increase his speed or walk with very short steps:

The mirroring (*Rectus* or *Inversus*) of a theme can be compared to the feelings of a man who stands on his head. His blood runs to his temples, his breathing rate is reduced, and he must find a new centre of equilibrium:

101

The Secret of Creative Art

Cancrizan is an inverted retrogression through the notes of a theme. It produces alterations of position, orientation and progression, similar to those experienced by a man who is obliged, without looking back, to travel a well-known route in the opposite direction:

(b) The expressive use of intervals.

Inversions of interval induce changes of effect. The step of a fourth g' to c' (bars one to two) gives tension, implying an increase of excitement or a *crescendo;* but the answer in the alto voice changes the energy of the subject as well as the subject itself. The downward step of a fourth g' to d' in bars two to three tends to weaken the tension.

In bar four the tenor's sudden repose aids the bass entry to stand out. It enriches the texture but does not complicate it. At this point the second half of the introduction begins. The alto inversion (three quavers from the end of bar five) reduces the compass in all voices at bar six. Not only does it decrease the independence of tenor and bass, but indirectly helps to bring out the real answer.

At the beginning of the piece, the two voices confine themselves mainly to the interval of a sixth enclosed on the one hand by the octave and on the other by the second. This allows the parts to move in both directions and maintains the effect of tension (bars two and four).

Descending themes gain in power by inversion, so much so that a melody which starts with a fall has the effect of a bridge passage (see tenor and alto at bars eleven to twelve).

Neatly-ended themes give an impression of purpose when moving downwards, but in upward movement they have an interrogatory effect. If the straightforward and the inverted forms follow one another their results are in contrasted moods (bars twenty-two to twenty-five).

Bach's Last Composition

(c) *The spacing and its emotional effect.*

Once only does the part-spacing embrace three octaves: this is in bar 29, at the entry of the third line of the chorale. The melody too passes through its greatest range at this point; its compass embraces an octave. The piece here reaches its emotional climax, and the fact is underlined by the soprano reaching its highest, and the bass its lowest note. The four voices reduce their compass at the end of the chorale entry to its smallest spacing, that of an octave (bar thirty-two, third beat).

At the end of the chorale's first strain, the spacing covers two octaves; at the end of the second entry only a twelfth. At the end of the third, it is compressed into one octave, and only recovers its normal range of two octaves at the final pause. The tense quietude which accompanies the flow of the chorale prelude is thus reflected through the whole structure.

At the end of the piece, the feeling of spacing vanishes with a force that is almost symbolic. The tenor stops in bars 42-43 while the alto embroiders the melody of the upper voice. An entry in the bass (bars 43-44) adds to the tune a mysterious character due to its depth in pitch. Final references to the theme flicker throughout the texture in the last bar.

(d) *The significance of the thematic structure.*

This is shown most clearly in the role which Bach assigns to the first four notes of the tenor theme ('Vor Deinen Thron'). They introduce every entry of the chorale, with the exception of the last line (bar 8, alto and tenor; bar 19, the same; bar 29, alto and bass). Elsewhere the phrase is found as the answer in the bass (bar 8) and in the tenor (bars 9 and 10): in the bass (bar 19), in the alto and bass in thirds, and the bass alone (bar 20). At the climax of the piece, in the third line of the chorale, the tenor has the phrase and then the bass (bar 30), and its rhythm is present in the thirds at bar 31. Finally the phrase drops out

103

altogether after the start of the last entry of the chorale (bass and tenor, bar 41).

There is a veiled reference to the first phrase in the countersubject at bars 2 to 4:

It is generally present and makes an unexpected appearance in the alto, moving in thirds above the bass entry between bars 4 and 5:

The tune of the fourth section (bar 34) disentangles itself in an inverted diminution that is almost mystical:

(e) Bach's expressive use of textural variation.

This is very markedly shown at the entries of the chorale. All four produce an unearthly atmosphere, in that the chorale is intoned in note values of twice and often more than twice those of the voices below.

At bar 6 the reduction in part-spacing produces the effect of exhaustion. After the sombre plagal cadence in bars 10 to 11, on the other hand, the texture is illuminated by the single remaining tenor voice.

Bach's Last Composition

The slow imitative writing at bar 14 eliminates any feeling of lightness.

The individual timbre of each successive entry at the end of the second section of the chorale increases the intensity, not only of texture, but also of expression. The significant change of texture, when the bass inverts the tenor motive in bar 38, suggests the utter resignation of the personal self.

III

Bach's imaginative use of polyphonic imitation.

First section: bars 1 to 7.
(Text: 'Vor Deinen Thron tret' ich hiermit').

The tenor entry is inverted at the octave by the alto whose descending steps have a weakening effect, where the tenor seemed urgent and decisive. The bass answers at the fifth in bar 4, followed as before by its inversion in the alto. The passage thus consists of two equal halves of three and a half bars' duration.

Spacing and emotional tension merge at the beginning of the second half. The compass is enlarged to a tenth, and each of the three voices achieves complete individuality. At bar 6, they divide into a melodic alto with accompaniment in tenor and bass. The cadence (bar 7) eases the emotional tension.

The tenor sings: 'Before Thy Throne, O God, I stand'. The whole section breathes a mood of tranquillity and total surrender. External nuances (such as crescendo or rubato) are valueless. All emotional stimuli have found expression in melodic contour and perfect spacing.

The inversions at the octave always occur a bar after the entry of the theme, and in this way the latter impresses itself on the mind.

The Secret of Creative Art

Second section: Sixth quaver of bar 11 to bar 18 inclusive.
(Text: 'O Gott und bitt' demütiglich').

The inverted entries follow twice as quickly as before, after only half a bar (bar 12). Where before they occurred at the octave, now the interval is reduced by more than a half to a fourth. Three entries follow one another in succession, instead of two only. All this points to an increase of tension. This is further confirmed by a cadence that holds up the first half of the section (bar 14). The first real answer follows at bar 15, and, like that in the bass at bar 4, it begins at the fifth (but this time on the fifth degree of the melody, to correspond with the tensional increase).

The answers in bars 12 and 13 occur at the fourth and third respectively. An inverted entry in the bass (bar 15) reduces the contrasted parts to a relationship of melody and accompaniment. This second section, larger than its predecessor, falls into divisions of three and a half and four and a half bars' length. In place of the harmonic cadence in the seventh bar, bars 17 and 18 introduce a melodic cadence.

The appropriate text is 'And humbly pray with outstretched hand'. Meditation heightens to emotion and the original mood only comes back with the cadences at bar 18.

Third section: bar 22, sixth quaver to bar 29.
(Text: 'Wend' Dein genädig Angesicht').

As in the first section, a whole bar elapses before the theme is inverted. This time four entries follow one another: tenor, alto, bass and, at bar 25, tenor again.

The entries occur at the fifth, octave, and fourth, thus recapitulating the fourth-fifth-octave relationship characteristic of both halves of the second section.

Bach's Last Composition

The tenor subject is self-contained and modulates at both the inverted entries. The section at once turns into the subdominant minor (bar 25).

This section does not divide into two equal parts, as did the first. It falls into divisions of five and two bars. The tension is released with the return to G major at bar 27. A bass entry follows at the fourth but in relation to the inverted tenor lead of bar 25, remains at the octave. By now the climax seems to be over, and the intensity decreases.

The words belonging to this passage are 'Turn not Thy face away from me'. They seem to induce the expressive climax of the piece, suggesting Bach's contrast between present self-consciousness and 'Losing oneself in God'.

Fourth section: bar 32, fourth beat, to bar 42, third beat.
(Text: 'Von mir betrübtem Sünder nicht').

This section lasts seven and three quarter bars, as compared with the seven bars of the first and third, and the eight bars of the second section. Its component phrases separate clearly into divisions of five and a quarter and two and a half bars long. The tenor phrase has the same note values here as the chorale tune.

Six entries are successively made: tenor, alto, bass; tenor (bars 34 to 35), alto and tenor. The answer in the alto is at the fourth, the bass entry at the second. The tenor follows at the sixth, and is answered at the seventh by the alto. The tenor then closes the section with an entry at the octave of the preceding alto lead.

In the second half (bar 38 onwards) the answer is in the tenor at the fifth above. The alto enters a third above it, its relationship to the bass entry being a seventh.

The final tenor entry (bar 40) is identified with the previous bass lead by its occurrence at the octave.

107

The Secret of Creative Art

The two main leads (bars 33 and 38) and the tenor's final answer are in the relationship *rectus—inversus—rectus*. The circle closes and the inversions bring the subject into congruence with itself.

The voices tend to lose themselves in the theme and succeed each other at very small distances of only three quavers, as opposed to the other sections where the entries follow each other after eight and four quavers respectively.

The text is 'A wretched sinner though I be'. Man is united with the infinite and his consciousness fades in becoming aware of his unity with eternity.

It was no accident that the technique of imitative counterpoint lay in abeyance after Bach's death. The audacity needed for its practice was too great for later composers. The simple application of thematic treatment, as in symphonic music, had first to be developed. Contemporary music, however, has returned to imitative technique as to a charm. In this connection twelve-note music may well be carefully studied, for in it the genius of Arnold Schönberg has effected the reintroduction of this technique at a most appropriate time.

To search for 'formalism' behind the 'science of living' is to misunderstand the nature of music. The mere use of the latter to fill out form, on the other hand, is a sin against aesthetics, for the processes of imitative counterpoint imply vital alterations to the basic material and original impetus of music itself.

Bach's last chorale prelude strikes at the roots of man's physical, psychological and spiritual being. It can only be understood with reference to the special circumstances under which it was composed. In this work creative ability becomes perceptible, even during the struggle for physical existence.

In listening to this music, one is aware of stimuli far beyond human realization. Bach's last composition demonstrates abilities whose superhuman nature renders them only accessible to genius.

III

The Imaginative Portrayal of Musical Material

(Ludwig van Beethoven)

'But though our outward man perish, yet the inward man is renewed day by day.'
(2 Corinthians, iv. 16).

Although Beethoven was deaf, in the imaginative treatment of sound he has no rival. He could apply his creative powers to music with far greater freedom than any other composer. Perhaps because of his deafness, his musical life was deeper than that of others more happily endowed. This misfortune and these gifts are shown alike in Beethoven's nine symphonies.

His technical processes become clearer with each fresh study of his work, until his artistic life reveals to us how his imagination penetrates even the most elemental principles in music. He used the mechanics of sound with a rare insight until the art of music appeared as a higher and more mature organism than ever before.

Imaginative Portrayal of Musical Material

THE INDIVIDUAL CHARACTERISTICS OF ORCHESTRAL INSTRUMENTS AS EXEMPLIFIED IN BEETHOVEN'S NINE SYMPHONIES

'That he should think of his miserable fiddle, when the spirit is speaking in me!' Beethoven's rebuke to Schuppanzigh is an admirable demonstration of his attitude towards instruments.

Beethoven, like Bach, was a viola player in his youth, and thus acquired a thorough knowledge of the instrument's peculiarities of tone and techique. By the time his deafness began (1798), he knew Mozart's operas and last three symphonies, Haydn's Masses and last twelve symphonies, as well as the music of the French revolution: (Cherubini, Méhul, Grétry and Gossec, whose *Tuba Mirum* for distant wind band had already appeared). Thanks to these and to the highly developed solo literature for all instruments (Bach's Chaconne was published in 1798 in Cartier's *L'Art du Violon*), the groundwork had been laid for an appreciation of every instrument's particular timbre and virtuoso capabilities. Beethoven completed this work and revealed instrumental qualities hitherto unsuspected. He also devised new orchestral effects by translating extra-musical stimuli into technical possibilities. This work was so thorough that Beethoven's exposition of instrumental technique and effects has remained the foundation of orchestral composition.

1. The Woodwind.

Beethoven enlarged the compass of music. Until then it had been naturally bounded by the limits of the human voice:

He set himself to enrich both lower and higher registers.

Characteristics of Orchestral Instruments

In the tenor solo of the Ninth Symphony he took the double-bassoon down as far as:

and the piccolo as high as

In addition Beethoven darkened the bassoon's B♭ by using the ghostly beat of the bass drum, an instrument of indefinite pitch:

Bassoon
Double-Bassoon
Bass Drum

while raising the piccolo's highest note with the thin pitchless sound of triangle and cymbals:

Piccolo
Triangle
Cymbals

To recognize the genius with which Beethoven widened the road from the perceptible limits of the piccolo's and double-bassoon's pitches towards infinity is to receive an amazing insight into the secrets of artistic creation.

The Flutes.

(a) Piccolo.

The piccolo and double bassoon were originally excluded from pure music, as were the trombones, triangle, cymbals, bass drum and harp.

111

Imaginative Portrayal of Musical Material

Pure instrumental music should be free not only from a text but from any instrument of essentially theatrical or otherwise evocative associations. But Beethoven used a piccolo, trombones and a double bassoon as early as in the Finale of his Fifth Symphony, if only to match its immense feeling of tension with a corresponding instrumental compass, to increase the orchestral brilliance and to deepen its powers of expression.

To the piccolo Beethoven allots:

(a) stormy triplets

(b) brilliant virtuoso scales:

(c) a sparkling trill which starts piano:

These three uses of the piccolo—for expressive tension, technical brilliance and stimulative force—were superbly shown by Beethoven.

In the storm in the Pastoral Symphony, the piccolo serves almost exclusively for purposes of colour. Only fifteen sustained notes are entrusted to it, but they so impress themselves on the orchestral fabric that they seem to drive it forward to the climax and dominate the whole expressive medium:

The Ninth Symphony finally finds the piccolo piercing the sound of the Hymn to Joy with an incorporeal march-rhythm:

The perfect execution of this task still demands the most brilliant technique of the orchestral musician.

(b) *The Flute.*

Beethoven's nine symphonies determine once and for all the use of the flute. Every nuance is there exemplified both for virtuoso and expressive cantabile purposes.

Imaginative Portrayal of Musical Material

Beethoven distinguishes between the various degrees of staccato for:

(a) triplet figuration, as in the First Symphony (Andante con moto)

(b) delicate fluidity as in the Third Symphony (Scherzo, allegro vivace)

(c) ethereal brilliance (Finale, allegro molto)

(d) spring's awakening as in the Fourth Symphony (Allegro vivace)

(e) distant fading of sound as in the Sixth Symphony (bridge passage between the storm and the shepherd's song)

(f) relaxation of tension as in the Seventh Symphony (Vivace)

(g) bucolic dance rhythms (Allegro con brio)

114

Characteristics of Orchestral Instruments

(h) acrobatic lightness as in the Eighth Symphony (Allegro vivace)

Similarly the legato was profoundly explored and used for:

(a) the soft euphony of G♭ major—Third Symphony (Allegro con brio)

(b) high, passionate singing (Finale, allegro molto)

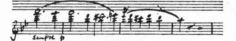

(c) melodic tracery of an indeterminate character, Fourth Symphony (Allegro vivace)

(d) broadening a melody, with movement over a full pianissimo (Adagio)

By an association of ideas Beethoven inspired new possibilities of technique such as:

(a) sighing semiquavers in a high register. Third Symphony (Marcia funebre, adagio assai)

(b) rising syncopated lament (Marcia funebre)

(c) the droll crack of a whip, Sixth Symphony (Allegro ma non troppo)

(d) calling triplets (Allegro)

(c) *The Oboe.*

It was left to Beethoven, in his deafness, to discover the intensity of the oboe's piano which can sound through the whole orchestra. Its soft cries in the C minor funeral march variation for wind from the Fifth Symphony

are heard as penetratingly as are its plaintive sighs over the pulsating semiquavers in viole and violoncelli during the same movement.

116

Characteristics of Orchestral Instruments

Beethoven calls on all the oboe's expressive powers in the Adagio recitative from the first movement of the Fifth Symphony,

though its consolatory character had previously been fixed in the major episode of the funeral march from the Third Symphony.

The Pastoral Symphony adds to this the role of the child-like voice of nature:
Sixth Symphony (Introduction to the shepherd's song)

As early as 1800 Beethoven had presented the oboe as the bearer of tense foreboding:

later he developed the expressive use of the minor key, as in the Second Symphony (Larghetto):

or in the coda to the funeral march of the Eroica where it illuminates the texture of these closing bars with a gentle sostenuto A♭.
Third Symphony (Marcia funebre):

Imaginative Portrayal of Musical Material

(*d*) *The Clarinet.*

The conception of the clarinet as the richest and most adaptable instrument in the orchestra is almost entirely due to Beethoven. Music did not previously contain such sounds as this above a double-bass pedal:

Fourth Symphony (Adagio)

Nor, before Beethoven, was the clarinet entrusted with the profound introspective calm of:

Fourth Symphony (Adagio)

nor the deep meditative concentration of:

Sixth Symphony (Andante, molto mosso)

This newly-found richness of sonority carried with it, too, a corresponding increase in expressive use of the clarinet's cantabile. This is exemplified in the expressive dialogue between clarinet and horn:

Seventh Symphony (Allegretto):

and again in the canonic use of clarinet and bassoon for expressing
the intimacy of folksong-like melody:

Fourth Symphony (Allegro vivace)

The clarinet is also called on to whisper a pianissimo melody in the
key of D♭:

Eighth Symphony (Allegro vivace e con brio)

The clarinet is also called on to whisper a pianissimo melody in the
It attains an almost superhuman character in this answering call:

Ninth Symphony (Adagio molto e cantabile):

The protean versatility of the clarinet is nowhere better illustrated
than in the varied effects which it produces from similar notes and
figures. In the first example the figure drops like tears from the
melody on the oboe:

Third Symphony (poco andante of the Finale):

In the second it babbles good-humouredly underneath:

Fourth Symphony (Allegro vivace):

Imaginative Portrayal of Musical Material

The Fourth Symphony first gave to the clarinet the opportunity for displaying constant virtuosity, which later caused it to adopt the role of first violin in the military band:

Fourth Symphony (Allegro ma non troppo):

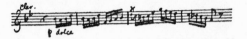

Lastly, Beethoven showed its picturesque powers of characterization when, in combination with the bassoon, it produces an effect of formal charm:

Sixth Symphony (Allegro ma non troppo):

(e) *The Bassoon.*

The eighteenth century was the first to take the bassoon seriously as an instrument of virtuosity. Beethoven added to this its place as a messenger of wit and gaiety.

The considerable and contrasting compass characteristic of the bassoon (ranging from the growling bass-notes through the melancholy baritone register up to the pinched and nasal high notes) was not merely used by Beethoven for new effects but as an ideal medium for intensifying musical expression.

In our first example the staccato notes of the bassoon cherfully mark out the tonality:

Second Symphony (Scherzo Allegro-Trio):

120

Characteristics of Orchestral Instruments

But in the next passage, it chases the violins with a waggish humour that is all its own:
(Allegro molto):

In the Fourth Symphony the staccato crotchets beat out the arpeggio of B♭ with delightful animation:
Fourth Symphony (Allegro vivace):

Below, the bass notes unconsciously rectify the oboe's drunken rhythm, with a heavy snoring wit:
Sixth Symphony (Allegro):

Lastly the sforzati on the bassoons in the Eighth Symphony make game of the would-be polished rhythms of the horns:
Eighth Symphony (Tempo di menuetto, Trio):

The expressive tone colour of the bassoon was Beethoven's discovery. It stretches from a frightened pianissimo:
Fourth Symphony (Adagio):

Imaginative Portrayal of Musical Material

to thirds of mournful charm (Allegro vivace):

and the cooing of turtledoves (Un poco meno allegro. Trio):

In the next symphony the bassoons are cast in roles of breathless suspense:

Fifth Symphony (Andante con moto):

and of questioning melancholy: (Andante con moto):

It is significant that Beethoven saw the bassoon in this passage as an instrument of almost human declamatory power.

He was particularly fond of the bassoon, and gave to it some of the most good-humoured touches. The scurrying semiquaver theme entices bassoon, clarinet, and lower strings one after the other to play the soloist, a part particularly unsuited to the last.

Fourth Symphony (Allegro ma non troppo):

(a) Bassoon

(b) Clarinet (see first example on page 120)

(c) Celli and Basses

Beethoven's ingenuity in the art of musical abstraction is shown in the bassoon 'quotation' from Mozart's G minor Symphony. The strings' legato version of the theme is here daringly changed into staccato chatter on the bassoon whose pauses threaten to break it up. Fifth Symphony (Allegro):

Beethoven then uses the pinched high notes of the bassoon to give the impression of stifled escape from the theme.

2. The Brass.

Despite his deafness Beethoven's creative conception enabled him to discover musical sonorities hitherto unknown.

(a) The Horn.

Beethoven invented for the horns an effect in pedal passages which has been in continuous orchestral use ever since:
Ninth Symphony (Adagio molto e cantabile):

Imaginative Portrayal of Musical Material

To him we owe the greater range of expression achieved by presenting a theme in dialogue for several instruments:

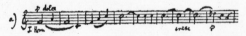

Lastly he turned the horn into a virtuoso instrument of almost limitless capabilities.

He employs it for fine rhythmic pointing:
Ninth Symphony (Molto vivace):

In the next quotation the horn's low growl unifies the orchestral texture:
Third Symphony (Marcia funebre, Adagio):

Time after time he varies its expressive use
(a) pastorally
Third Symphony (Allegro con brio):

Characteristics of Orchestral Instruments

(b) heroically:

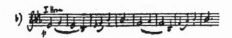

(c) oratorically (Finale, poco andante):

The second horn's low pedal Bb has an effect of inky melancholy:
Fourth Symphony (Adagio):

The horns can also supply a theme with implications of approaching climax:
Fifth Symphony (Allegro con brio):

With similar implications Beethoven also entrusts them with the high fortissimo statement of this rousing theme:
Seventh Symphony (Allegro con brio):

In the Eroica the horn's character changes from the sound of a bugle to that of Nature herself and, ever since, it has been connected with the width and depth of a distant view and the mystery of twilight in the woods.
Third Symphony (Scherzo, Trio, Allegro vivace):

Imaginative Portrayal of Musical Material

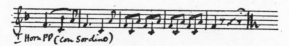

The Pastoral Symphony closes with a pianissimo muted horn solo whose performance calls for real virtuosity and expressive delicacy: Sixth Symphony (Allegretto):

In his last symphony, Beethoven confronts the horn player with a passage of almost superhuman stature. It rises from the depths of the human soul and displays the full sonority of the instrument: Ninth Symphony (Adagio molto cantabile):

(b) The Trumpet.

By comparison with his treatment of the horns, Beethoven's trumpets are used fairly conventionally. Nevertheless the trumpets are used with particular ingenuity in the Funeral March from the Eroica. Here, at the climax in A♭, their bleak unison sounds like the crack of doom:

This innately tender treatment of the instrument bears little relation to the biting wit entrusted to the trumpets in the Pastoral Symphony. Here with a lordly gesture demanding a stop to the revels, the 'master of ceremonies' requests the entrance fee from the dancers before the amusement can continue:

Sixth Symphony (Allegro):

The finest example of rhythmic virtuosity is found in the second trumpet's pianissimo call from the 'military band' variation:

Ninth Symphony (Alla marcia. Allegro assai vivace):

In marked contrast is the effect of the vigorous trumpet rhythm which is repeated eight times, crescendo. A satisfactory execution of this passage calls for intensity as well as masterful self-control:

Third Symphony (Allegro con brio):

Imaginative Portrayal of Musical Material

(c) The Trombone.

Beethoven gives the trombone a superhuman character. Its powerful call breaks up the rhythmic drive of the Scherzo in the example below, and thus changes the music's character from the restlessness of D minor to the peaceful major at the beginning of the Trio:

Ninth Symphony (Molto vivace):

In the passages below three trombones underline the cadence at the climax of the recapitulation and later their heroic tones blare through the peak of the coda.

Fifth Symphony (Allegro):

In the last example the bass-trombone, like the voice of eternity, leads the male chorus in intoning the words:

'Seid umschlungen, Millionen.'

Ninth Symphony (Andante maestoso):

3. The Drums.

Beethoven transformed the timpani from being merely a means of rhythmic dynamism and textural accentuation into an instrument of virtuosity and expressive power. This was one of the most amazing applications of his musical imagination. From then on, the drums became a father to the orchestral family, with powers of regulation, differentiation and concentration. They achieve a high degree of technical virtuosity and an almost limitless potentiality for rhythmic pointing.

Beethoven mingles distance and proximity through the drums. He uses them to accomplish the apparently remote modulation from:

to:

by means of the common enharmonic note B♭—A♯:

As the harmonic progression moves further and further away from B major the eddying drums roll distantly on, pointing the way to B♭ major. Fourth Symphony (Allegro vivace):

Imaginative Portrayal of Musical Material

They are used too to retard the end of the same symphony's slow movement. The solo timpani tap out the violin rhythm for the last time, giving it an atmosphere of uncertainty:

Fourth Symphony (Adagio):

These refinements, derived from the most stubborn material, show Beethoven's real genius in the application of musical mechanics.

The timpani take on an almost human expressiveness, as the figure

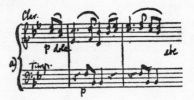

defines the phrases of the melody:

Ninth Symphony (Adagio):

(a)

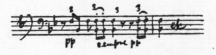

and later, where the euphony of the fifth:

(b)

130

Characteristics of Orchestral Instruments

moves naturally out of:

On the other hand Beethoven employs the drums to release the destructive forces of nature from their bonds.

Ninth Symphony (Allegro, ma non troppo, un poco maestoso):

Concertante passages are found, as in:

(a) the coda of the Scherzo in the Eroica

or (b) the bouncing octave intervals

which mark Beethoven's first use of something other than tonic and dominant tuning:

(a) Third Symphony (Scherzo, Allegro vivace):

131

Imaginative Portrayal of Musical Material

(b) Eighth Symphony (Allegro vivace):

Later, octave tuning is reintroduced rhythmically. This passage calls for virtuosity of the highest order.

Ninth Symphony (Molto vivace):

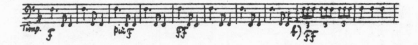

Technical innovations always furthered Beethoven's emotional expression. Thus the crescendo repetition of the leaping rhythm at (b) of the above example drives the music towards its climax.

Just before the Finale of the Fifth Symphony the pianissimo string chord of A♭ is interrupted by an elusive attempt to beat out the rhythm of the main theme on the timpani:

Twice this is almost achieved; then the rhythm becomes so embedded in the ear of the listener that the drum repeats only the first of the triplets, reducing the motive to:

Then it is lost in a maze of fluid sound.

Characteristics of Orchestral Instruments

From this point to the spate of energy that erupts in the terrific drive of the Finale, the music exemplifies that superb coolness under the fire of creative phantasy, which Schubert described as the mark of Beethoven's genius.

Fifth Symphony (Allegro):

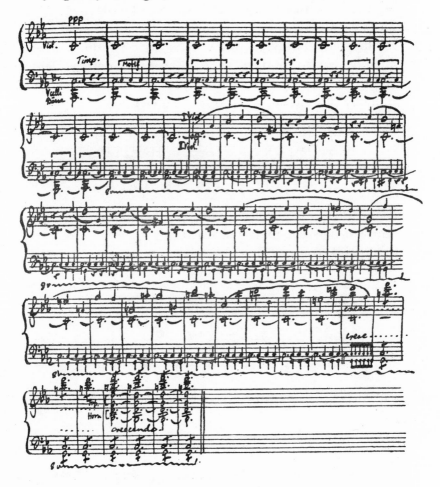

Imaginative Portrayal of Musical Material

THE INTENSIFICATION OF MUSIC'S STRUCTURE

Beethoven revised all the basic elements of music: metre and rhythm, thematic material and melody, harmony and the use of intervals. He brought all these to a perfection previously unimaginable and loaded them with a tension that is still vivid to-day.

He transformed mechanical counting into the very heartbeat of his music. He did not merely compare metre with rhythm; indeed, in the example below, he contrasts them so that the metrical definition of the first beat is broken down by the persistence of rhythmic sforzati. First Symphony (Menuetto, Allegro molto e vivace):

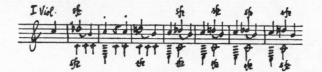

Beethoven also developed peculiarities of the division of bars which gave to music a new polymetric character.
(Andante cantabile con moto):

Metre as a time-resisting feature is contrasted with rhythm lost in the flow of time.
(Menuetto, Allegro molto e vivace):

The Intensification of Music's Structure

1a. Metre.

Beethoven's imaginative treatment of metre began with the First Symphony. The work begins with a V⁷—I cadence in F major. The chord of F becomes a subdominant triad in C major, and is followed by a V—VI progression which interrupts the cadence on a chord of A minor.

The dominant chords in bars one and two should both occur before the beat. Instead they stand on the metrical strong beat of the bar, thus shifting the harmonic strong beat, in each case, from the beginning to the middle of the bar.
First Symphony (Adagio):

The whole of the third bar is, harmonically speaking, one up-beat, and the metrical structure is made clear only with the V⁷—I cadence in G, now doubly confusing harmonically. Meticulous dynamic indications (Fortepiano-piano, fortepiano-piano, piano-crescendo-forte) underline the intentional ambiguity. Despite the **Adagio** calmness which pervades the start of the C major Symphony, a fundamental inquietude is immediately communicated to the listener.

During the first movement, there is a more sombre passage in G minor into which Beethoven inserts contrapuntally two melodic phrases, of contrasted metrical construction. The bass line is eleven bars long, and seems to split up naturally into phrases of four, three, three and one bar's length. The woodwind entry at bar three changes its character; three bars for oboe are followed by three in which it is joined by the bassoon in the lower octave. The passage closes with three cadential bars. This brings about the following contrasts in melodic phrasing between bass and upper parts:

135

Imaginative Portrayal of Musical Material

$$
\begin{cases}
\text{Bass:} \\
\text{Upper part:}
\end{cases}
$$

| Bass: | 1 2 3 4 | 1 2 3 | 1 2 3 | 1 |
| Upper part: | 1 2 | 3 1 2 | 3 1 2 | 3 |

Bar number: 1 2 3 4   5 6 7   8 9 10 11

The ear unconsciously attempts to mollify the resultant contradiction with a new conception of the bass.

Bass: 1 2 3   1 2 3   1 2 3   1 1

This contrapuntal interlacing of differently constructed phrases enabled Beethoven to increase the metrical tension.

First Symphony, first movement. (Allegro con brio):

The second movement shows Beethoven's peculiar application of metrical contrast. A simple 3/8 signature has the aural effect (see the second example on page 149):

1	2	3	1	2	3	1	2	3	1	2	3
1	2	1	2	1	2	1	2	1	2	1	2
Str.	W.	Str.	W.	Str.	W.	Str.	W.	Str.	W.	Str.	W.

In this way its natural flow undergoes slight but perceptible variation. In the third movement Beethoven uses the contrast between straight phrase structure and arbitrarily accented melody to develop a new kind of tensional increase.

The Intensification of Music's Structure

The repetition of the theme is marked by sforzati in the following way: four plus three bars / two plus two plus three bars. The accents then fall at intervals of two bars, one bar and four times again every bar. The shortened versions of the theme contradict one another and increase the emotional momentum to such an extent that, when the pianissimo subito breaks in, wind and timpani try twice to replace the order of the classical four bar phrase (see example 1, p. 150). Then the theme breaks free again and closes quickly with phrases of two and four bars length:

In the fourth movement, Beethoven succeeds, as he so often did later, in suspending the value of the bar line altogether.

Three times the strong beat is quietly overstepped by running semiquavers. The fact is the more difficult to appreciate, since the semiquavers start almost inaudibly after two pauses which have considerably shaken the feeling of tempo. The wind joins in the third of these runs, at the octave, inducing an effect of power and certainty which the violins, pianissimo at bar four, further accentuate.

At bar six, this pianissimo reverts to piano, and the phrase is marked staccato instead of legato. In this way the second of the three bar phrases becomes the up-beat of the returning principal subject. The eight bars of the latter, reacting against the nuances of phrasing described above, divide neatly into groups of one, two and five bars' length. As, however, the five bar phrase splits up into two and three bar phrases, the subject shows its clear connection with the semi-quaver movement that followed the pauses.

Imaginative Portrayal of Musical Material

Tutti:

The metrical refinements, described above, from the First Symphony give an idea of the broad road trodden by Beethoven in his subsequent symphonies: it culminates in the Scherzo of the Ninth Symphony, with its concise simplifications of barring and witty individual relationship between phrases of three and four bars' length.

1b. Rhythm.

In the Second Symphony, forerunner of the Ninth, Beethoven first uses his later technique of developing a whole work from one single rhythmic phrase, or of constructing a movement on one single figure.

The rhythm of the opening Adagio's first phrase :

plays a similar structural role in the Introduction, the Larghetto and the Scherzo. It pervades the Introduction, whether as the sighing upbeat figure of the strings:

138

The Intensification of Music's Structure

or as the falling woodwind figure: —

In the opening melody of the Larghetto its value is of a bar's duration:

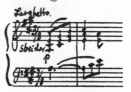

and its presence is felt in both the secondary themes in E major:

Imaginative Portrayal of Musical Material

Finally the sixteen-bar theme of the Scherzo grows out of it.

Beethoven's groping, almost semi-conscious efforts in this work were to turn, in the Fifth and Seventh Symphonies, to intentional expressive treatment. The almost incomprehensible uniformity of the C minor Symphony springs from the inexhaustible opportunities for development offered by the implications of its rhythmic motive, just as the massive inner compactness of the A major Symphony is due to the basic rhythm which carries along all its four movements.

Fifth Symphony in C minor: Principal motive 2/4.

Its appearances and transformations in the first movement:
(a) uncertain in direction:

(b) employing contrast by movement in different directions:

(c) clear and direct in aim:

The Intensification of Music's Structure

(d) forming a theme:

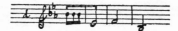

(e) intensified by complementary use of rhythm:

(f) increased in vigour (the triplets altered to duplets):

 is more forceful than

Second Movement:

(a) counting out the last beats of the theme and in augmented values:

(b) underlining the closing phrase in two forms:

(c) in diminished form, intensifying the strings' up-beat:

Imaginative Portrayal of Musical Material

(d) carrying the subsidiary theme:

(e) loosening the tension of its accompaniment:

(f) pulsating through a held note:

Third Movement:

(a) driving the theme in the bass:

(b) shaping the horn theme:

(c) pulsating through the melody of the trio:

(d) played on the timpani, as if remembered:

The Intensification of Music's Structure

Fourth Movement:

(a) as an energizing component of the main theme:

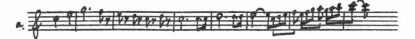

(b) and of a subsidiary unison passage:

(c) as an invigorating accompaniment:

(d) in a diminished form, ascending:

(e) as a thematic element of the second subject:

(f) accentuating the feeling of coda:

Imaginative Portrayal of Musical Material

Seventh Symphony in A major

First Movement:

I. Basic rhythms:

II. Theme:

III. Component elements of the theme:

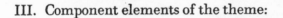

Second Movement:

I. Basic rhythm:

II. Limited, in accompanying form, to:

III. Reduced in the coda to:

The Intensification of Music's Structure

Third Movement:

I. Theme:

II. Component elements of the theme:

III. Basic rhythm of the Trio:

IV. Augmented and inverted melodic version:

V. Telescoped and diminished form in the accompaniment:

Fourth Movement:

I. Basic rhythms:

Imaginative Portrayal of Musical Material

II. Theme:

III. Constituent parts of theme:

2a. Motive.

Listening to music is a synthetic experience of art. Independent of whether the music is perceived consciously or unconsciously, the listener has to hear a piece in its entirety so that he can understand it as a whole. Every note of the composition has an instructive as well as a constructive value.

The thematic material is thus the factor of chief importance. Beethoven's rhythmic and melodic treatment of themes forms the nucleus of the 'didactic' technique of composition, which he brought to maturity.

Although this technique of composition has much in common with the older art of variation-writing, it is not the same. It was rather a successor to the structural principles of the classical symphony.

The external unity of the suite pattern was due to the employment of a single theme, which served as material for all the movements. The organic unity of the symphony on the other hand results from the contrasted treatment of several themes, as in sonata form, so that principal melodies develop new basic characteristics in different movements and tonalities are varied by means of cadences.

Didactic composition replaced variation form through the metamorphosis of pure instrumental composition into a key-stone of creative art.

The Finale of the ballet, *Die Geschöpfe des Prometheus* op. 43

The Intensification of Music's Structure

(first performed in 1801) begins with the same theme as the Finale of the Third Symphony (composed between 1802 and 1804). In 1802, Beethoven again used the theme for his 15 variations and fugue for piano, op. 35.

In these three works we find Beethoven, during four of his most fruitful creative years, again and again using the same theme as a basis for variation and chaconne treatment.

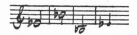

But it was only in the Finale of his Third Symphony, written after the publication of Bach's Chaconne for solo violin (in Cartier's *L'Art du Violon*) that Beethoven arrived at the principles of symphonic structure which best corresponded to his creative abilities.

In the first three movements, the theme remains considerably under the influence of the old suite form. It is only at the end of the work that the principal subject is isolated and becomes the core of the Chaconne that forms the Finale:

In the Finale it takes its place as the foundation of the most monumental of all sets of orchestral variations:

It is only here that the formal idea of the work, as prodigious as it must have been novel, can be properly appreciated. The first three

147

Imaginative Portrayal of Musical Material

movements are like huge reflections of one and the same basic image; the Finale presents the theme of the Chaconne, in retrospect, as the structural basis of all four movements of the symphony.

The following analysis of the variations gives a comprehensive idea of the thematic treatment which Beethoven here brought to complete fruition for the first time.

The Intensification of Music's Structure

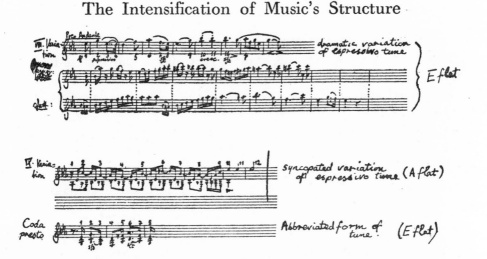

These analytical examples recall inevitably the Finale of Mozart's Jupiter Symphony. The difference lies in the way the two composers mould their material. Beethoven, like Mozart at the end of the Jupiter Symphony, employs strict triple counterpoint in his seventh variation. But where Mozart's technique causes the listener to abandon himself to the power of the climax, Beethoven forms his multiple themes consciously and from necessity.

A fascinating feature of Mozart's Finale is that it gives an audible impression of simplicity despite its wealth of strict counterpoint. Its real polyphony illuminates, but is smoothly subordinated to, the main melodies and the counterpoint seems almost an end in itself. In just those passages where the imaginative possibilities of counterpoint begin to be unfolded, their appearance causes the formal idea of the movement to take a secondary place. In Beethoven's work this is never allowed to happen. His pre-occupation with increase of intensity was forever refining and clarifying the expressive potentialities of music.

It is therefore not surprising that the strict counterpoint which he applied to the Finale of the Eroica falls more easily on the ear than that of the Jupiter Symphony: that, in fact, the ear becomes oblivious

149

of it in the face of the music's formal intensity. One of the best examples is the start of the expressive tune in the double-fugue (Variation 7).

The metrical alterations undergone by this theme are not, as in the Jupiter Symphony, merely the result of contrapuntal development, but conscious methods of increasing expressive tension:

Beethoven here uses serial variation form as an aid to composition. The notes of the theme appear unchanged but metre, rhythm and compass undergo considerable alteration.

Another example of Beethoven's serial variation form is found in the eighth variation, in which the expressive melody is announced in a declamatory form that greatly increases its emotional effect. The technique finally appears as the basis of the ninth variation where complementary rhythms transform the passionate character of the theme into one of sighs and fears.

2b. Theme.

Beethoven's instrumental themes are quite different from those of the other great composers. The more brightly his genius burned, the more he simplified the structure of his melodies until he found his ideal in the Ode to Joy from the Ninth Symphony.

This melody had to be so written that it realized Schiller's invocation to the listener: 'Wer ein holdes Weib errungen, stimm' in unsern Jubel ein.'

The Intensification of Music's Structure

The considerations governing the formation of such a melody were as follows:

1. The theme must be at once memorable; in other words, it must impress itself on the audience at first hearing.
2. It must be within the compass of every voice.
3. It must be uncompromising in the quality of its musical, aesthetic and expressive content, so that its popularity value never outsteps the limits of fine art.

The developmental process, which culminates in this melody, finds its starting point in the First Symphony. Here is the theme of the second movement:

If the first note is transposed up an octave, the nucleus of Beethoven's instrumental themes may be seen. In each of his symphonies he strove to find its ideal formation: fine melodic structure of a folk-like character, immediately memorable: limitation of compass to that of any speaking voice (in this case the sixth) and an inner structure of tenderness that is not found in melody in its rulgar forms.

The melody of the Trio of the Second Symphony foreshadows the form perfected in the Ode to Joy.

In this tune Beethoven's three requirements seem to be almost flawlessly fulfilled.

Let the following examples speak for themselves:

Imaginative Portrayal of Musical Material

The impressive ease of these melodies is due to their symmetrical structure. The same limits of compass bind them on both sides in constantly novel rhythmic tension. They are all alike, but each has its own structural characteristics.

These themes, taken from the nine symphonies have another characteristic in common: they are closely related to each other. Almost all have an identical harmonic basis, and the melodic structures follow corresponding lines.

To illustrate this the examples are given again below, this time transposed into the same key:

The Intensification of Music's Structure

3a. The Interval.

Beethoven rediscovered the function of intervals as the support of melodic and harmonic progression. He revealed all their inherent capabilities, and applied his own imaginative design to their structural implications.

The purposeful aspect of music is as clearly demonstrated in the Fifth Symphony as anywhere. Its first movement bristles with active tension. How is this connected with the use of interval? Strangely enough it is through the limitations imposed by the smallest interval used in the music. The decisive interval is in this case the minor third. The rhythmic germ of the work: ♩♩♩ is governed almost exclusively by it. Occasionally seconds and fourths replace the third:

On the other hand the unnoticed intervals that join statements of the basic motive increase from the second via the fourth and sixth to the diminished fifth and seventh and eventually the octave.

The perfect fifth retains an almost exclusively downwards movement, which gives it the function of a dominant resolution. The fourth however moves in both directions, stating, and connecting statements of, the main theme, and maintaining the equilibrium of the tension.

Whenever intensity increases, the minimum interval takes first place. This is certainly true of the tremendous emotional concentration at the climax of the development.

Beethoven here decreases the size of his minimum interval, gradually replacing the major by the minor, augmented and then diminished second and eventually moving enharmonically on to a unison. The pulse of the music seems to halt, as the movement of the intervals is reduced to mere repetition of the same note:

Then the neutral fourth comes again into prominence, this time as the basis of the brief contemplative oboe recitative:

The second and most intense climax of the movement is entirely brought about by movement through the smallest interval. Diatonic seconds, the third connected with the main theme, and powerful repeated notes, all contribute to the mounting tension and to the terrific peak when fifteen unison Gs are hammered out by full orchestra:

The steely pounding of the first movement comes from the unbroken use of small intervals unsubdivided below the minor third.

The Intensification of Music's Structure

The yearning character of the second movement is however due to the perpetual subdivision of large intervals and their resolution by diatonic step:

The two themes of the third movement:

are equally contrasted. The ghostly pianissimo upward movement of the first melody begins indeterminately with a fourth, gropes its way up the C minor arpeggio and hesitantly drops a fifth by way of a third and second. It then collapses on to the fifth G, which is repeated twelve times fortissimo by the horns. The repetitive nature of this subject and the way in which it is concluded rely on the same small intervals that Beethoven had previously used in the first movement.

This contrast between groping harmonic impulse and repeated monotone induces the most vast of all the tense crescendi that Beethoven wrote.

· This method of disorganizing a theme was quite new. It wanders aimlessly round its central point (G) six times. The fifth is not recognizable as the directive interval, but the theme develops from it, climbing to the octave by means of the minor sixth and seventh while, in the lower register, basses and timpani beat out the repeated pedal note until the resultant impetus reaches an explosive climax. The determined thirds which open the last movement decrease at once to the smallest diatonic interval of a second. Later in the broad jubilant theme:

sixths and sevenths replace it.

Beethoven's new-found art of interval treatment is excellently illustrated by the descending fourth figure, eight times repeated and quoted below. The first and second runs together drop a sixth, as do the third and fourth. But, while the fifth and sixth twice attack the same note, runs seven and eight at last achieve the octave. In this way, the intervals are filled out, directed and joined to intensify the significance of the passage.

Enlarged intervals increase expressive power. This is shown below by the growing compression of intensity brought about by movement from the third to the fifth, and later from the fourth to the sixth and octave:

Contracted intervals increase energetic tension. This is shown by the repeated notes in the accompanying bass of the passage above.

Intervals repeated as if in stretto announce the approach of a climax. An illustration of this will be found in the mounting repetitions of the theme quoted at the bottom of page 154.

The Intensification of Music's Structure

3b. Harmony.

Beethoven's sketch-books contain only sparing indications of harmonic scheme. While he refined the rhythmic and melodic structure of his themes incessantly, his sketches pay scant attention to their harmonization.

The harmonic basis of his motives must therefore have presented no problems to Beethoven, unless the harmonic scheme of his symphonies was fixed without reference to melodic formation.

The themes of the symphonies move in every case over the simplest harmonic ground. Secondary chords and plagal cadences play little part in them.

Harmony is merely the scaffolding over which Beethoven's melody and figuration can, within well-defined limits, move freely without tiring the listener. He only once tried to work differently; in the first subject of the Eroica Symphony, a theme which might almost be called primitive:

The theme bears more resemblance to those in his other symphonies if it is reduced to its simplest terms (bars 1—4 and 9—12); but even so, it is obvious that Beethoven would never have allowed himself to start a symphonic work with such a rudimentary and constricted theme.

The harmony at bar 5:

would seem aurally to give the first chord of the movement a retro-spective implication of dominant harmony, for the ear hears the C♯ at this point as a D♭ despite the absence from the chord of E♭ or E. The resultant indecision of tension removes some of the clarity charac-teristic of Beethoven's themes. This is counteracted by the introduc-tion of emotionally contrasted dynamic markings of a precision to be found nowhere else in his symphonic themes:

bars   5   6   7   8   9   10   11   12

        p cresc. sfz   sfz—p   cresc.   p

Each of the nine symphonies has other harmonic peculiarities. In the First Symphony, the first, third and last movements all start outside the main totality of C major. All three movements use the dominant G major as an individual contrast, which gives a new directness to the C major that eventually follows.

The Intensification of Music's Structure

In the First Symphony, the problem of starting the movement is solved harmonically. By contrast with Mozart's and Haydn's treatment of the introductory adagio (Mozart with a solemnity that mounts to the subsequent allegro, Haydn with the contemplation that comes from spiritual retrospect), Beethoven sets himself a purely musical problem. By veiling the main tonality at the beginning, he sets up such an expectation in the listener that the entry of the real tonality, and so of the movement proper, follows on like the natural release of accumulated tension.

The second problem posed in the First Symphony was the replacement of the conventional minuet by the scherzo.

Beethoven marks the movement Menuetto (allegro molto e vivace, $\downarrow$.=108), in order to make the nature of his innovation quite plain. The form is thus really that of the old minuet with trio. But the spirit, like the tempo, is altogether new.

Here, if anywhere, Beethoven's dictum, so well revealed in his own work, is manifestly intelligible; that it is rewarding to impregnate the old forms with a modern poetical outlook.

Beethoven's third movements abandon the function that Haydn gave to the Minuet, that of a realistic dance-like form and a fitting contrast to the spiritual point of repose found in the Adagio. Henceforth the Scherzo is an integral part of the whole symphonic structure and carries the urgent rhythmic energy of the first movement through to the Finale of the work.

Neither Minuet nor Trio of the third movement in the First Symphony have anything in common with the dance movements of Haydn and Mozart.

In the C major Symphony the Scherzo begins in G major, growing from piano to forte as it announces the theme.

This is followed by the second half of the Scherzo, a figure of three notes:

Imaginative Portrayal of Musical Material

which, in an abbreviated form, passes rapidly through E major, C minor, A♭ major, G♭ major and D♭ major. After a brief pause, the first two notes of the figure bring back the main tonality of G major by means of B♭ minor and G♭, and the recapitulation begins.

The Trio in particular delighted Beethoven's contemporaries, some of whom likened it to the trembling of the Aeolian Harp's strings. It is, in contrast, built on the simplest of harmonic progressions. The second part indeed, which consists of eighteen bars, is only made up of melodic phrases based on the chord of the dominant seventh, and moving no further than the ninth.

The Scherzo and beginning of the Trio are seen in a more clearly contrasted light at the Scherzo da capo, which resumes its function of tensional increase with an effect that is all the more stimulating.

New and significant tonalities (G major melody in a scherzo in C); quick passage through distant keys (as cited above); simple, lingering harmonies (in the middle of the Trio). These were the harmonic features of his new scherzo form.

As in the general treatment of symphonic structure, Beethoven's first two symphonies are less concerned with solving problems of harmonic refinement than with preparing and introducing them.

One of his most important discoveries is found in the introduction to the Second Symphony; this is the way in which Beethoven anchors his harmonic progressions during the bridge-passage to the movement proper.

160

Thus, between D and B♭ major, he writes:

and again, between B♭ major and D minor:

while between D minor and D major occurs this passage:

Similarly, in the development section of the first movement, after a piano statement of the second subject, the harmony climbs from G up to C♯ major by means of a fortissimo outburst from the whole orchestra:

The climax of the first movement is equally induced by purely harmonic conglomeration:

Imaginative Portrayal of Musical Material

An even more intentional and urgent use of harmonic structure occurs at the climax of the second movement just before the recapitulation:

In the first bar of example (b), page 161, occurs the altered chord:

sharply modulating from B♭ to G major. As time went on, Beethoven more and more frequently employed simple and complex altered chords of this kind to signal the various turning points and climaxes. Thus the trebly-altered chord:

occurs, dynamically underlined, in the fourth movement of his Second Symphony:

In the second movement the texture is abruptly darkened by major-minor modulation, a device which Beethoven was later to use with such remarkable effect:

The Intensification of Music's Structure

The Trio, too, contains a famous example of an audacious key-change:

The process of narrowing down the thought to one ambiguous dimension finds its complement in the apparently illogical harmonic movement of line in the first movement of the Second Symphony:

The Third Symphony, the Eroica, marks the first appearance of Beethoven's new symphonic form, though its ultimate structure is only found in the Ninth Symphony. (First movement: Exposition without repeat; second movement: Scherzo in place of Adagio; third movement: impersonal melodic climax of the work, not self-expressive movement; fourth movement: dialectical development in place of Finale or conclusive solution of symphonic problems).

In the Eroica the form at last becomes symphonic in the modern sense, themes assume new and forceful proportions, rhythms forge the movements and chords are revealed as instruments of construction.

The significance of harmonic scheme, from the Eroica onwards, is best demonstrated at the recapitulation of the principal subject.

Imaginative Portrayal of Musical Material

In the fifth bar, the harmony over C♯ in the bass introduces E in lieu of the missing E♭, thus strengthening the stimulation of the crescendo in bars 5 and 6.

The F major tonality which follows in bar 7 and the pastoral horn passage which it introduces are all the more satisfactory. The new-found power of harmony is here made manifest, as it was first formulated by Rameau: 'Harmony alone can rouse the passions. Melody saps them of their vitality.'

The unexpected resolution on to F major of the preceding chord:

opened up a new world of sound and expression.

It was in the Eroica, forty years before Wagner, that Beethoven first introduced the chord of the ninth to underline an emotional moment. It appears here in almost all its possible manifestations:

harmonic:

melodic:

linear:

as a dissonant
appoggiatura:

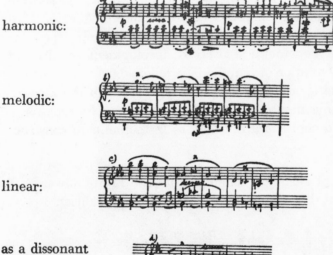

as a resolving *appoggiatura:*

intensifying:

realistic:

climactory:

The intensification of musical vocabulary in the Eroica sharpens the harmonic effect.

Beethoven develops in this work, among other things, a new treatment of anticipation and suspension.

In the example below, the dissonances are made to seem intentional by their presentation fortissimo as harmonic anticipations.

165

Imaginative Portrayal of Musical Material

In contrast, when used pianissimo, they increase the tension to just within breaking point.

The harmonic suspensions below, in restraining their resolution, tend to be heard as independent groups of sound.

By enharmonic change in the bass the accumulated energy of the diminished seventh is suddenly released, through harmonic logic, and becomes a dominant seventh.

The logic of harmony thus finds itself for the first time in the Eroica Symphony.

It enables Beethoven to use dissonance with a retrospective effect of tension (as is also the case at the beginning of Wagner's *Tristan und Isolde*). The acoustic severity loses its acerbity in the harmonic resolution that follows, and is recognized as a constituent part of the whole musical mass:

The Intensification of Music's Structure

This dissonance is a characteristic harmonic element of the symphony, and one which Beethoven gradually develops. It corresponds to that which starts the Finale of the Ninth Symphony, and which is formed by 6/3 chords in D minor and B♭ where the fifth of the D minor triad later becomes the bass of a dominant chord:

The introduction to the Fourth Symphony lays stress on the use of the diminished third (G♭ and E, formed from G and E♭ in the key of B♭ major).

The strengthened intensity, brought about by free interpolation of the leading note, later gains special significance harmonically. A diminished minor seventh accompanies the use of this chord, first on the fourth degree of the scale,

though later, like the Neapolitan sixth, it was applied to other degrees.

The chord of the ninth is almost more important in the Fourth than in the Third Symphony. It occurs in more and more new ways; only two can be shown here. In the Scherzo, chords of the ninth ($F^{9♭}$, $G^{9♭}$, $C^{9♭}$, and $F^{9♭}$) are used successively for linear contrast:

while in the Finale, the chord appears in the main theme's melodic structure.

The process of integrating or superimposing elements which should follow one another in succession, plays a great part in the Fourth Symphony. It is this process which brings about the euphony of the pedal chord, A^{7b} placed over an anticipatory $B\flat$ in the bass:

A contrasted example of this device occurs in the fourth movement where
$$E^{7b} \quad \text{and} \quad F^{6b}_4$$
are combined fortissimo. Here the anticipatory tonic chord in second inversion breaks imperiously through the pulsating diminished seventh with a demanding 'Halt'.

But the significant feature of the Fourth Symphony lies in the use of violent harmonic contrast. An example of this is found at the beginning of the introduction, when the chord of the sixth in $B\flat$ minor (i.e. $G\flat$) makes a sudden enharmonic change to $F\sharp$, and in place of $B\flat$ minor, a magical dominant minor ninth on $F\sharp$ is heard:

The Intensification of Music's Structure

The next example provides us with one of Beethoven's most subtle harmonic ideas. It shows the enharmonic broadening of

and its return to B♭ after alternating between the two chords:

The passage flows dreamily over a pedal B flat (=A sharp) on strings and timpani.

It is interesting to note that this passage is worked out simultaneously by linear and harmonic means.

At the end of the Fourth Symphony Beethoven returns to the serial variation technique previously found in the Adagio of his Eroica Symphony;

but here for the first time he is working in purely linear terms. The straightforward harmonic scheme is thereby considerably heightened in effect, and the final cadence, following the *a tempo* gains correspondingly in power:

If the Third Symphony took the decisive step in unfolding the architecture of Beethoven's symphonic form, the Fifth shows his design at its most self-disciplined. Every problem posed in the music receives the most forceful and concentrated solution possible.

Diminished and dominant sevenths here replace the chord of the ninth. Instead of broad harmonic planes, he uses hurrying and ambiguous movement. Continuous mounting tension gives way to massive energetic restraint. In place of expressive harmony, Beethoven makes novel and mysterious use of homophony.

The First and Second Symphonies begin Adagio and move gradually into the Allegro.

The Eroica, after two full chords, leaps straight into the process of shaping the musical material.

The Fourth Symphony returns, though by new methods, to the broad Adagio introduction.

The Fifth concentrates into two unison phrases the whole energy of the work.

At the beginning:

E♭ would seem to be the tonic. But it is soon followed by:

with a pause on the D, which seems to point to B♭ major (suggesting a possible harmonic progression IV-I). The piano section in C minor, however, makes clear retrospectively the harmonic logic of the two previous outbursts:

Surely never before in the history of art had humanity been so 'roared at' and 'called to attention' as at the beginning of the C minor Symphony!

This technique of summoning the listener and demanding from him a maximum of concentration corresponds, in a negative sense, to the interrupted cadence before the Finale, which breathlessly sums up all the forces previously released.

If in the first example the listener was degraded to the position of a mere acoustically sensitive object to be dominated by the eruptive overflow of the beginning, the effect of the passage quoted below should be quite opposite. The expectancy which the tension, at that point, prolongs to unbearable limits, should activate him in the extreme:

The reason for this is found in the harmonic progression:

Here the second chord can neither be interpreted as the chord of A♭ (for the fifth is missing) nor as the tonic triad of F minor (for there is no F).

171

Imaginative Portrayal of Musical Material

The climaxes are more strongly marked in the Fifth Symphony than ever before. The chord of the ninth is replaced by simple and diminished chords of the seventh. The dissonant notes, therefore, that imply a chord of the dominant minor ninth in the example below (9^b and 7), gain doubly in effect when, at the entry of the G, they change into martellato repeated thirds:

Diminished sevenths follow one another quickly, and the sharpened leading note characteristic of this chord adds urgency to the approaching climax:

This urgency brusquely guides the movement and assumes a deliberate character by the simultaneous use of enharmonic change and double harmonic alteration:

In the second movement, Beethoven makes use of the chord of the diminished seventh on the leading note (in E♭, the dominant of this movement's key), and thereby greatly increases the melodic expressiveness of the passage. Here the woodwind gently move apart, but their resultant harmonies are interlocked.

172

The Intensification of Music's Structure

In the Andante con moto, the dominant seventh is even used as a means of limiting the energy of the movement.

Twice the orchestra hammers out the scale of E♭, as if to modulate, and ends on a held fortissimo E♭. Then over the same note, the dominant seventh enters pianissimo moving towards A♭ until, with a final shudder, forte, of the diminished triad on the leading note:

it dies away.

In the coda of the same movement the dominant seventh is again used to tone down expression, though the restricting effect of the diminished seventh on the leading note makes the process of emotional collapse seem more evident.

Both the examples that follow demonstrate Beethoven's novel use of harmony to achieve an atmosphere of mystery.

A fortissimo chord of C major on full orchestra is answered by horns and trumpets with the third E-G, while the root of the chord continues to sound until it fades quite away. The third is taken up by pianissimo strings and becomes the bass of the diminished seventh E^{7}♭. By means of enharmonic modulation, chromatically altered passing-notes and double suspensions, the first chord moves, through

$E_{4\flat}^{6\flat}$, $D_{5\flat}^{7\flat}$, to $D\flat$, $D_{4\natural}^{6\flat}{}_{3\flat}$, $C\flat^{6\flat}$, $E\flat$ and finally $A\flat$ major. Thus it achieves in retrospect the harmonic status of:

The breathtaking power of this passage is well contrasted with the rhythmic pulsation of the example below.

The trumpets hold a C through eight harmonic progressions:

the movement proceeds from $G\flat$ to $B\flat$ minor (by way of a Neapolitan sixth):

With tentative steps:

the harmonic structure moves to $G\flat$, or rather $F\sharp$ minor:

But this progression proves insufficiently forceful in itself, and is again altered, this time to the first inversion of D major:

The Intensification of Music's Structure

In the progression described above, the sliding first inversions:

move tentatively from D♭ major to the distant key of G♭ minor in search of a definite tonality. The effect is temporarily to extinguish, but eventually to intensify Beethoven's particular powers of harmonic reasoning.

With the process of concentration and self-discipline completed in the Fifth Symphony, Beethoven was now ready to embark on that of deepening and simplifying (though not trivializing) his musical material. This work was begun in the Sixth, and achieved in the Ninth Symphony, where the complex and the straightforward are at once combined.

The two intellectual ideas in the Pastoral Symphony represent the peaceful landscape as nature's passive, and the thunderstorm as her active side. The implied contrast is between the shepherd's and the peasant's use of nature and man's contemplation of her. Beethoven was here presented with an opportunity to simplify his music by treating it, as painters would say, in broad washes of colour.

The idea of melody in broad washes provides an explanation for the astonishing harmonic treatment given to the two main subjects of the symphony's first movement; it consists of a constant repetition of the dominant-tonic cadence:

Imaginative Portrayal of Musical Material

The theme of the Scherzo is treated in part even more simply. The first half employs only simple tonic harmony, and it is not until near the double bar that the relative minor is reached:

Other themes too, in this symphony, revolve round plain harmonic cadences, among which the V-I progression is by far the most common.

The storm scene alone appears to be more richly harmonized and, as if to compensate, each chord is prolonged over several bars:

This harmonic expansion is symbolized by the 'bagpipe' chord characteristic of the symphony:

Beethoven starts the work with this open chord and develops the first movement from it; in the Finale it achieves a new sonorous and emotional expansiveness. At first it only appears in drone form:

and over it the melody adds its second constituent fifth:

The Intensification of Music's Structure

This combines subdominant, tonic and dominant in one chord together with their modulatory tendencies in both directions, and the resulting broadening of expression:

The elasticity effected by this use of the open ninth is made clear when its constituent notes are added:

The tendency of the open major ninth (F_5^9) is to reduce the mass of sound to its bass note F. For this reason, Beethoven treats the chord as a combination of dominant seventh and tonic harmony. The tonic pedal has a similar tendency to absorb the whole melodic plane above it.

This example is of special significance, for Beethoven here uses the pedal point not only as a central force, but also as a negative element which compresses vertical harmony and horizontal melody into one dimension.

Nature in her active state alone, as represented by the storm scene, is rich in dissonances. The section begins with brisk jerks from D♭

major to E♭ minor and F minor.:

The effect of the passage is enhanced by a number of modulations into remote keys.

The preparation of the climax is particularly interesting. It is accomplished by the harmonic progression:

these two diminished sevenths are sustained for several bars at either end of the progression, so that they act as harmonic anchors. The outbursts in F major, two of which occur in the same cadence, give to the second of the chords (F♯$^{7♭}_{♯3♮}$) an enharmonic implication in retrospect of G♭$^{6♭}_{2♮}$ and the salient chords are thus heard as a logical progression:

in the key of F major, VII$^{7♭}$ (E$^{7♭}$)—III$^{7♭}$ (A$^{7♭}$).

The Intensification of Music's Structure

Beethoven's struggle for simplification and self-discipline, as shown in his extremist treatment of sonority and expression, cannot here be too much admired.

The three middle symphonies (nos. 6, 7 and 8) are endowed, to some extent, with similar functions.

If the Sixth may claim to be typified by a predominant chord, the Seventh is equally characterized by a predominant cadential progression, while the Eighth develops Beethoven's new pointilliste technique of harmonic extremism.

The Seventh Symphony is dominated by an unflagging impetuosity. A similar feeling of urgency marks the lead from the introductory Adagio into the Allegro, from the Scherzo into the Trio and from the third movement into the Finale. This intimate connection between constituent sections and even movements of the work is accomplished purely by means of harmony.

Beethoven gives a totally new significance in this symphony to the ordinary V-I cadence, by preceding the chord of the dominant, at each point of climax, by the triad on the flattened submediant.

The work begins with a quiet melody, based on the harmonic triad, over a decrescendo cadential figure that quickly reaches F major. But as soon as the chord is heard it assumes the status of a flattened submediant triad in A major. This gives the succeeding dominant harmony an expansive character not usually associated with the simple dominant-tonic relationship.

The sequence is repeated just before the Allegro, but this time there is a crescendo from pianissimo to fortissimo between the submediant and dominant chords.

Imaginative Portrayal of Musical Material

The Scherzo too incorporates this cadential sequence indirectly into its theme, with stimulating effect:

The effect is gentler but none the less remarkable when the Trio fails to make use of the characteristic cadence, but instead employs the F major third, A, as a pedal and modulates into D major:

At the end of the Scherzo however, the composer corrects himself. The sustained A heralds a reminiscence of the Trio, in D major and minor and the A then returns fortissimo to its original place as the third of the characteristic progression $VI_{\natural}^{\natural 5}$-V-I:

The Intensification of Music's Structure

But the melody definitely returns to F major at the end, which would seem to disprove any possibility of the use of the characteristic cadence:

To reason thus, is to isolate the third movement from the rest of the work. The F major chord is seen in a wholly different light as soon as the Finale starts; for the chord of E major connects the F major of the Scherzo with the A major tonality of the last movement by means of the same characteristic cadential progression.

The sole function of harmonic extremism is to reveal the romantic side of every day occurrences, as in the Fourth Symphony.

Most of all the technique needs humour, arising from use of the unexpected. Musically it corresponds to the desire for simplification which becomes more and more marked in the last four symphonies. This simplification brought with it a more profound use of musical material; it did not therefore limit Beethoven's aims to mere concentration but brought out, in addition, the subtle many-sidedness of his musical ideas.

In the Seventh Symphony Beethoven inserts general pauses to facilitate the appreciation of his unprepared modulations:

181

Imaginative Portrayal of Musical Material

He returns to this technique in the Eighth Symphony. The first subject rushes headlong and fortissimo from F major on to a dominant seventh in E flat, in its second inversion:

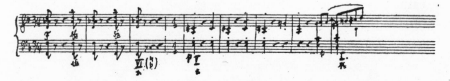

After a general pause of two bars, this moves hesitantly, and in the manner of the Seventh Symphony's characteristic cadence, on to a cadential 6/4 on the dominant of D major:

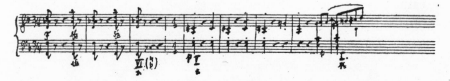

This method of replacing energetic tension by pointed wit and formal gesture is well shown in the above example. It is paralleled by several other passages in the Eighth Symphony which strengthen the impression that Beethoven was here releasing a totally new technique of musical repartee.

Whereas the themes of Beethoven's other symphonies are to some extent defined, almost all those in the Eighth lose their way, like the one quoted above. By way of compensation their beginnings are, by a simple harmonic structure, all sharply marked.

The second subject of the first movement begins in D major with three melodic sequences, rising over ordinary I-V, I-V progressions. Then somehow the theme loses its thread melodically and harmonically, only to start confusedly again in C major, as one does after forgetting the point of an anecdote.

The Intensification of Music's Structure

The point of the second movement is wittily driven home when, after wandering round in several keys, the riddle comes to an end in the key nearest its own, i.e. the dominant of the passage in question:

The Finale is marked by elaborate musical punning.

The first subject sprints lightly into the dominant and stops there. As if striving to escape, the orchestra blares out the chromatically lowered submediant, notated as C♯ (instead of D♭) following the inverted cadential progression I-V-VI♭, and then gaily starts the theme again.

The first two appearances of the second subject are interrupted on the chromatically lowered submediant (inverted cadential progression again). The effect recalls Jean Paul's phrase about 'unexpected wonders in broad daylight.'

This theme too is very simply harmonized. But as in the example cited above, it never comes to an end. Instead, it simply repeats the beginning, side-steps from A♭ to C major, and helplessly begins again a third and fourth time.

Just as the Eroica excelled all previous symphonies in mass and imaginative power so for sheer monumentality, considered as the culminating point of Beethoven's formal development, the Ninth surpasses even the Eroica.

In a certain sense too, it provided a starting-point for the formative achievements of Stravinsky, Hindemith and Schönberg.

Stravinsky's polyrhythm has in this work a prototype of unrivalled excellence.

The first few bars of the Andante moderato section of the third movement lack a metrical strong beat, allowing the melodic line to flow on in happy self-oblivion.

In spite of this, the metrical structure imperceptibly replaces the rhythm, and this is due to exceedingly delicate preparation in the preceding Adagio. Twice the new 3/4 time-signature appears in it, first silently on the strings, then taken up in turn by horns, double-basses and celli:

Beethoven thus combines the following three rhythms within the metrical structure:

It is not until the fourth bar that the melodic strong beat releases momentarily the theme from its metrical suspense.

The strangely powerful affirmation of the tonic that closes all Hindemith's recent works has also its prototype in the Ninth Symphony. Certain passages in the last movement avoid all reference to D major, in order that the tonality of the work may return, in each case, with increased brilliance. These passages are here tabulated together with their metrical duration.

90 bars

(Introduction—as far as the first statement of the principal theme by lower strings)

112 bars

(Double fugato in the development section, from after the tenor solo in B♭, 'Froh, wie seine Sonnen fliegen' to the return of the main theme, note against note in the chorus)

61 bars

(Male- and full-chorus, from 'Seid umschlungen Millionen' in G major to 'Uber Sternen muss er wohnen')

32 bars

(From 'Ihr stürzt nieder, Millionen' to 'Muss ein lieber Vater wohnen')

19 bars

(From the Poco Adagio in E major for solo quartet, 'Alle Menschen werden Brüder' to the last choral prestissimo)

This intentional emphasis on the tonic is found in all Beethoven's symphonies.

Thus we find:

at the end of the first movement of the First Symphony, a C major fanfare lasting 21 bars;

at the end of the last movement of the Second Symphony, 11 bars of repeated D major;

in the Finale of the Eroica, a statement of E♭ major 19 bars long;

at the close of the first movement of the Fourth, 8 assertive chords of B♭;

29 bars of jubilation in C major at the end of the Fifth;

even in the level harmonic scheme of the Pastoral, F major chords of 7 bars' duration;

only the Seventh brings back the home tonic by means of a plain
V-I cadence;

the Eighth returns to the tonic again and again with an F major
orgy of 13 bars;

the end of the Ninth devotes 14 whole bars to rolling chords of
D major.

Despite the level plane of Beethoven's harmony in his symphonies,
they contain nothing so bound by convention as the dominant-tonic
beginning of Mozart's Jupiter Symphony.

Beethoven seems not only to have foreseen the chief harmonic
problem of contemporary music, the continual broadening of tonality
to a point of total relaxation, but to have wished to protect music
from it by every weapon in his armoury.

This harmonic problem leads straight to Schönberg. And in fact the
Ninth Symphony contains the first, almost flawless twelve-note series
at the words 'Ihr stürzt nieder, Millionen':

I can still remember, as a boy hearing it for the first time, the
inexplicable, enigmatic impression left on me by this passage,
feverishly groping its way up and down. I must confess to my shame
that I have only now discovered the reason for its strange effect.

The degree to which Beethoven carried his process of material
intensification is audibly shown in the start of the Ninth Symphony.

For fourteen bars the open fifth of A minor rolls up and down the
orchestral compass.

A more misleading introduction could not harmonically be
imagined. For the fifth A-E does not represent the key of A minor,

The Intensification of Music's Structure

but is a protracted building-up of tension towards D minor. The passage
announces a definite tonic, but moves away nevertheless towards an
unknown region, and this ambiguous character is strengthened by
the fifth A-E and its pulsating rhythmic progressions.

Beethoven rarely made his creative powers so clearly recognizable

as here. The repeated rhythm  moves incessantly on, and

right from the start its aim introduces a contrary tendency which the
open fifth tries to affirm as its own A minor, but which eventually
proves to be of dominant significance:

The contrapuntal contrast of harmony and rhythm in the above
example is, in later passages of the Ninth Symphony, replaced by
other contrasts that intensify the level harmonic scheme.

Thus the famous coda of the first movement is constructed over
fourteen bars of tonic-dominant cadential harmony. Its retarding
tendency is restrained by trumpets and drums who ceaselessly assert
the impetuous rhythmic figure of the beginning, and again by the
strings who support the structure with chromatic and diatonic steps
of the fourth from D down to A and back again.

187

Imaginative Portrayal of Musical Material

Beethoven's fondness for retarding the harmonic development is all the more indispensable in the Ninth Symphony, for passages occur in every movement where the tonality seems on the point of losing its grip. This can be most plainly seen in the Scherzo, where the harmonic flow descends by thirds, hurriedly searching for a cadential point:

The eighteen keys tabulated below are referred to briefly prestissimo, but not one of them has sufficient force to become the new tonality for which the music is searching:

C—A minor—F—D minor ‖ B flat—G minor—E flat ‖ C minor— A flat—F minor—D flat—B flat minor—G flat—E flat minor— C flat—A flat minor—E—C sharp minor—A.

But there is yet another reason why Beethoven's underlining of the tonic is indispensable. This is the increasing importance attached to abbreviated cadences. He does not only juxtapose the first and last chords of these, but actually combines them into one chord.

The cadence A^7-$C\#^{7b}$-$G\#^{7b}_{\natural}$-A^6_4 is left unfinished. Beethoven omits the dominant and moves straight from a 6/4 on A to the tonic.

The Intensification of Music's Structure

A more subtle form of this progression occurs in the Adagio, but here its effect is opposite. Where in the earlier passage the tonic was reached from a 6/4 without the intermediate cadential dominant in the example below, the chord of the dominant in G major is held and becomes the basis of a new tonality, achieved without cadential preparation. A wealth of subtle connection is revealed in this passage, as, for example, in the enharmonic alteration of the dominant seventh on F into the trebly altered dominant of D major, a change only appreciable in retrospect.

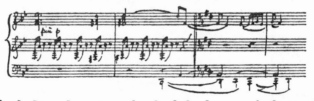

In the Ninth Symphony we also find the harmonic formation whose symmetrical construction (major thirds in both directions):

served indirectly as Schönberg's point of departure in his experiments with piled-up fourths, which are equally symmetrical in basis, having perfect fourths in both directions.

The augmented triad on the minor mediant is twice used in the following crescendo passage:

Imaginative Portrayal of Musical Material

and it is also the adopted tonic of Schönberg's First String Quartet in D minor.

It is thus easy to see how Beethoven's symmetrical construction furthered the harmonic urge to penetrate unknown ground, of necessity growing outside the old, regular conceptions of tonality.

But there is still another of the Ninth Symphony's innovations that must be mentioned. This is linear harmony, first developed by Beethoven in the Finale.

By this technique, the listener is himself faced with the problem of supplying horizontal recitative with a vertical basis, of recognizing three-dimensional harmony where there was before only two-dimensional line.

It was an act of optimistic daring to introduce linear harmony into absolute music, perhaps the most audacious act ever undertaken in the field of art. For, whereas the shorthand used by contrapuntists and thoroughbass teachers wanted only the imaginative co-operation of a realizer, Beethoven here trusts the listener—any ordinary person with an ear for music—independently and synthetically during the performance to direct the temporal formation of the music.

And the bass recitative must remain a senseless audible impression of deep rumbling to anyone who hears it and does not understand its harmonic basis.

The act of listening is here the act of collaboration. This was the modernistic revolutionary attitude adopted by the creative genius who saw himself not as the chosen prophet but merely as a deputy realizing what many others were equally capable of doing.

The Intensification of Music's Structure

With Beethoven's linear harmony, the wheel turned full circle. This would not have been possible without Sauveur's fundamental discovery in the field of acoustics; that a musical note contains in itself the natural phenomena of interval- and melodic-movement, harmonic and modulatory inclination, contrasts of intensity and timbre. And without it, Rameau could never have put into words his insight into the connection between all musical and aesthetic processes, the proof of which was, seventy years later, demonstrated in the orchestral recitative from Beethoven's Ninth Symphony.

Harmony alone can rouse the passions. Melody saps them of all their vitality.

CONCLUSION

To examine 'The Nature of Music' is to discuss the Nature of Man.

The new significance given to music after 1700 can be shown by repeating these three statements.

Sauveur's brief formula:

'I use the term *harmonic* for the sound which completes several vibrations while the fundamental completes one,'

Fontenelle's words:

'What philosopher would ever have believed that a body set in motion, all of whose constituent particles participate, nevertheless remains unmoved at certain points?'

and his final summing-up:

'This concept of the numerical proportions of notes is the representative expression of all the music that Nature has given us.'

Every sounding note could, by computing the sum of its constituent harmonics, be recognized as a chord, and melodic sequence be appreciated as coexistential harmony.

These were the views which formed the basis of accompanied modern homophony and renovated classical forms.

Both views were first consciously put forward in the eighteenth century, though, through the appreciation of music, mankind had for many years been unconsciously prepared for them.

The unity of melody and harmony, characteristic of modern European music, is the artistic equivalent of human refinement. As soon as man's spiritual forces were sufficiently mature for this amplification, 'Music laid the foundations; from them sprang the

Conclusion

perfected art form, and Beethoven used them as the material for his imaginative reforms.'

There is no music in nature without human activity.

Nature in itself possesses no musical elements or forms of its own, nor can it produce symmetrically vibrating strings or perfected reeds.

Nature lacks musical foundations and musical instruments. Its imperfection and asymmetry even exclude it from harmony.

Man's musical ear reaches beyond his state of life and far above nature.

It is one of man's faculties to perceive and make perceptible things which may at first be only ideals, even though they may have no corresponding sound effect in natural phenomena.

It was through this faculty that: 'a deaf mute discovered the scientific basis of music; that a blind and dying man first proclaimed the mysteries of its creation, while a third, also deaf, gave it an added emotional power.'

But music frees man from the terrors of mortality. It 'fulfils time', conveying to man the secret of vitality.

For what is melody—the strain of fleeting notes that, hardly living, die away again—but the wonder of existence itself: Birth, life and death?

To retain a melody in the memory is, for a moment, to conquer time itself. One single event in life and death is dead.

While sights of terror and destruction have inspired many masterpieces of painting and sculpture, music can never portray misery.

Music, after all, is not concerned with making life more beautiful; its function is to inspire the listener and to transport him beyond the limits of human existence.

For music is, by nature, positive.

This book is set in 12-pt. Walbaum, a design based on the group of faces referred to as ' Modern ' of the early XIXth century.

Justus E. Walbaum was born in 1768, the son of a clergyman. He was an engraver and caster of metals and at 30 started his own foundry. His designs were famous when he died in 1839.

The characteristic of the face is the squareness of the letters, particularly noticeable in the capital letters. Its accompanying Medium shows differences from the ordinary Roman, in the thick and thin strokes of *a*, and *e*. Walbaum is a distinguished type-face eminently suitable for books on art, poetry, music and philosophy.